PASSENGER TRAIN OPERATION

FOR THE RAILWAY MODELLER

BOB ESSERY

Ian Allan PUBLISHING

Front cover: LMS Class 2 2-6-2T No 41216 takes water at Hatherleigh on 9 July 1964 on the 10.38 Halwill to Torrington Service. *John Edgington*

Back cover, top: GWR 'Hall' class 4-6-0 No 6911 *Holker Hall* pauses at 17.45 at Par on 4 May 1959 on a Plymouth-Penzance ordinary passenger service. *John Edgington*

Back cover, bottom: LMS Horwich Mogul No 13004 departs Kendal Castle station on David Jenkinson's 7mm scale layout. *Tony Wright*

Title page: I believe this picture captures the spirit of what this book is all about: namely, passenger train services. I will never forget the day when, accompanied by a railway enthusiast friend, I caught a train at about midnight from Birmingham New Street to London so that we could see some of the early morning rail traffic in the capital. One of the stations we visited was Liverpool Street, and I was amazed at the number of trains that went into and out of the station. Although I cannot date this picture, I suspect that it is circa 1905 or slightly later. Note the Second Class branding on the carriage in the bottom left-hand corner of the picture. The locomotive, Great Eastern Railway No 1858 Claud Hamilton, was built in 1903. *Author's collection*

First published 2005

ISBN 1 7110 3157 6

Published by Ian Allan Publishing

an imprint of Ian Allan Publishing Ltd, Hersham, Surrey KT12 4RG.

Code: 0509/B2

Visit the Ian Allan Publishing website at:
www.ianallanpublishing.com

Contents

Glossary of Railway Companies		2
Preface		3
Introduction		4
1	The Development of Passenger Trains	6
2	Train Formation, Vehicles and Working Practice	22
3	Non-passenger-carrying Coaching Stock	38
4	Locomotives used for Passenger Trains	46
5	Passenger Stations	60
Postscript		95
Bibliography, References and Sources		96

Picture Credits

All illustrations are from the author's collection unless otherwise stated.

Glossary of Railway Companies

CR	Caledonian Railway		MR	Midland Railway
GCR	Great Central Railway		NBR	North British Railway
GER	Great Eastern Railway		NER	North Eastern Railway
GNoSR	Great North of Scotland Railway		NLR	North London Railway
GNR	Great Northern Railway		NSR	North Staffordshire Railway
GSWR	Glasgow & South Western Railway		S&DJR	Somerset & Dorset Joint Railway
GWR	Great Western Railway		S&MJR	Stratford-upon-Avon & Midland Junction Railway
HR	Highland Railway		SER	South Eastern Railway
L&YR	Lancashire & Yorkshire Railway		SE&CR	South Eastern & Chatham Railway
LB&SCR	London, Brighton & South Coast Railway			
LNWR	London & North Western Railway		**The 'Big Four' (post-1923)**	
LSWR	London & South Western Railway		GWR	Great Western Railway
LT&SR	London, Tilbury & Southend Railway		LMS	London, Midland & Scottish Railway
M&CR	Maryport & Carlisle Railway		LNER	London & North Eastern Railway
M&GNJR	Midland & Great Northern Joint Railway		SR	Southern Railway

Preface

A little over a hundred years ago, using clockwork toys, railway enthusiasts laid the foundations of the hobby that today we call model railways. Within a few years the first magazine dedicated to the hobby was published and since then countless thousands of words have been written about it. Notwithstanding the variety of subjects that commanded the attention of numerous authors, it seemed to me that one subject was badly neglected, namely the operational side of the full-size railway and how it could be reproduced in model form. It was this thought that prompted me to suggest to the publishers that there was a need for a book that would explain what happened on the full-size railway and to suggest what was possible in model form.

I am pleased to say that they agreed, and in due course *Railway Operation for the Modeller* was published. We took the view that it should have a wide subject range — I tend to use the term 'broad brush' — so that if it was well received by modellers we could enlarge upon selected subjects in later books. It soon became clear that many modellers welcomed this source of information and before long it was also clear that the two subjects readers would like to see in the next books were passenger train working and freight train working. We have therefore devoted a book to each subject, and in addition to covering the subject of the trains also examine the originating and terminating points for the respective traffics carried by the trains.

I would also like to acknowledge the work of Tony Wright who undertook the photography and to Warners Group Publications, publishers of *British Railway Modelling*, for allowing me to make use of the pictures in this book.

In preparing a book of this nature I am always conscious of the help that I receive from my friends, and in particular I would like to express my thanks to John Edgington for his very helpful suggestions and advice, without which this work would have been poorer.

In this book all the pictures of models were taken on the layout owned by the late David Jenkinson. David and I met in 1963 and we were friends for over 40 years. Although there were many aspects of railways, and in particular model railways, where we did not always see eye-to-eye, I had the greatest respect for his knowledge of carriages and passenger train working. But for his untimely death in 2004 there can be no doubt that he would have read the text and there is also no doubt that he would not have agreed with everything I have said. Therefore it seemed to me that one way whereby I could acknowledge our friendship would be to dedicate this book to his memory and to ensure that all the model pictures were taken on his Kendal Castle layout.

Finally, readers should note that I have tended to use the pre-1923 railway company names rather than post-1923 on the grounds that this is a more precise form of identification.

Bob Essery
Rolleston on Dove, 2005

This picture was taken at Wembley for Sudbury station in about 1949. It is quite likely that the train is an excursion train being run in connection with an event at Wembley Stadium. I think it captures the spirit of 'passenger traffic' rather well! *Real Photographs, courtesy of John Jennison*

Introduction

I n the Introduction to *Railway Operation for the Modeller* I set out my railway 'CV' so I will not repeat what was written in that book, other than to say that I have spent many years studying the working of the full-size railway and trying to reproduce it in model form. Indeed, I take the view that the best way the railways of yesteryear can be understood today, and in particular by those who never saw the steam railway, is by the use of accurate working models. However, there are problems.

The first is the widely held belief that you must have something happening all the time. While I can understand the demands of exhibition organisers who have to satisfy the entrance-fee-paying public, who just want to see the trains run continuously, such exhibitions can also be counter-productive to people like myself who wish to observe, in model form, the traditional steam railway and to savour those aspects that show that the builders know what they are doing. However, how can modellers who never saw the steam railway at work learn how it was operated?

In August 1968 the age of the main-line steam railway was over, and while steam power lingered on for a few more years on industrial lines, it was no longer possible to observe what was happening on the main line; you have to be over a certain age to have experienced it at first hand and to understand what was taking place. Furthermore it is not a subject that has commanded much attention from writers. If you ask modellers today about the subject of railway operation in model form, the only author who is widely identified with it is the late Frank Dyer, who, although not a railwayman, studied the subject very thoroughly and reproduced what he saw in model form in a remarkably effective manner.

It would also be true to say that in the past, in particular before World War 2, model magazines contained more features about various operational aspects than ever appear today, where the major emphasis appears to be on scenery or kit building. Indeed, at times I have felt that in the hobby it was more important to get the grass the correct shade of green than to ensure that the line was correctly signalled!

The object of this book is simple: to describe, in general terms, the evolution and development of passenger train services during the era of the steam railway and to try to show how it can be reproduced in model form. The subject is wide, so I have generally restricted this work to locomotives and rolling-stock, types of trains and methods of working, and a survey of different types of stations. Inevitably there will be some repetition of information from the first book, but I have tried to ensure that it is minimal and has only been included when absolutely necessary.

When selecting illustrations I have chosen to use pictures that do not show the final years of steam, and have included more from the 1930s

The Horwich Moguls, or 'Crabs' as they are usually called, were often used to work excursion trains, although on this occasion No 42901, from 26A Newton Heath, is hauling a scheduled working, the 8.30am Hull to Birmingham New Street express passenger train. Taken on 19 June 1954 when passing Beauchief signalbox, the eight largely Stanier Period 3 carriages are painted in British Railways carmine and cream and as such are representative of a secondary express train during the 1950s. *E. D. Bruton*

or earlier than from the BR era. There are two reasons for this: first, most modern books with an historical slant tend to have few pre-1948 pictures when compared with the post-1948 scene; and second, I think that pre-1948 is a more interesting period to model.

I have also tried to ensure that the balance of pictures and information sources is across all the British railway companies and not biased towards my favourite companies. Having said that, it is probably inevitable that I will use rather more Midland or LMS examples than those from other companies. This is simply because as a result of my interest in the railway companies that became part of the LMS group I am more able to quote examples of their practice than that of others. However, if your company is not Midland or LMS you can be sure that its working practices were similar, if not identical, although the GWR did tend to have its own way of doing things, and examples of that company's variations have been included. Generally, though, the basic rules and working practices applied to all British railway companies — it was only the details that varied. An example of this

common approach will be found in the section dealing with mixed trains in Chapter 2.

When I was undertaking research for this work I turned to *British Railway Operation* by T. B. Hare (see the Bibliography) and was delighted to read his remarks. His book was based upon a series of articles that had been published in *Modern Transport*, and Sir Ralph Wedgwood CB CMG, Chief General Manager of the LNER, wrote the foreword. This is what Hare had to say:

'It is very difficult to say exactly what should be the logical order of the different subjects which come under the general heading of railway operation. The whole thing is so interwoven that a knowledge of certain subjects which, from some points of view, should come late in the syllabus is desirable when discussing points which naturally have to be dealt with earlier.'

Although my words would be different from his, they would have a similar meaning — it is a question of where to begin. I freely accept that another author might use a different sequence from the one that I have chosen, but a decision had to be made and mine was to start with a review of the development of passenger traffic. I hope that readers will find this approach acceptable.

Before we begin to review the development of passenger traffic I would like to devote a little space to modelling attitudes and to consider how this can affect the models produced. The public side of the hobby can be seen at the numerous model railway exhibitions that are held almost every weekend throughout the country, and in the various model railway magazines that serve the needs of modellers. From these it is abundantly clear that the most popular era is the 1950s/'60s, and when the facts are considered this is perfectly understandable.

Although younger modellers are not old enough to have seen steam railways, other than the preserved kind, I suspect that the vast majority have some memories of the final years of steam from their boyhood years (and I am sure this also applies to many of those talented female modellers whose work has also graced the hobby from time to time). As a result, the image they have is of the final years of steam before 1968. This period is also largely featured in the majority of the prototype magazines, probably because there are more pictures from this era and this is the period that the contributors are able to describe. Finally, we should also remember that, since the hobby began, the trade has always concentrated on selling examples of the most modern engines in service, which does not make it easy for someone who wishes to model an earlier period of railway history.

I decided to put this theory to the test and to use my own personal experiences, which date back to the years prior to Nationalisation. I began to make models of railway subjects in 1946, but we can discount the early years. At first, until 1952, when for a few years I was not an active modeller, I used second-hand pre-war equipment or models that were 'freelance' in appearance, but in 1956 I started again in OO two-rail and have been active ever since.

My 1956 models were based upon the then current practice of the early years of British Railways; I could remember, and indeed joined, the LMS just before Nationalisation, but it was convenient to model what was the everyday 1950s scene. In 1960 I converted to EM and decided that my modelling period should be LMS, about 1937. The reason was simple: I was influenced by the writings of Norman Eagles, whose models were from this era. Looking back I suspect that his boyhood and formative years were during the 1930s, and this influenced his attitude and subsequent writing. In 1971 I decided to adopt P4 standards and once again changed my modelling period, but the influence was partly of my own making. For a number of years I had been working with the late David Jenkinson, researching the question of locomotive and carriage livery, and as a result I concluded that for an LMS modeller the period just after the 1928 livery change was more interesting than circa 1937. My P4 models reflected this

Top: One of the LMS 'named express' trains was the 'Thames-Clyde Express', seen here passing Dore & Totley South Junction on 19 June 1954. The locomotive, No 45573 *Newfoundland*, carries a cast-iron headboard, and in his notes the photographer says that all the carriages carried roof boards with the name of the train clearly displayed. *E. D. Bruton*

Above: Journey's end. This shows 'Claughton' No 6018 *Private W. Wood VC* at the head of the Down 'Lakelander' express approaching Kendal Castle station. The picture also shows the two trap points that were the subject of a long discussion between David and me when I sought to convince him that they were required to protect the passenger line alongside the platform. *Tony Wright*

period change, which saw the end of my interest in the Stanier era for modelling purposes.

Ten years later I changed to Gauge O, later adopting Scale 7 standards, and once again I went back in time, on this occasion to the mid-Edwardian years and the Midland Railway. This change was entirely the result of the research I had undertaken prior to writing *An Illustrated History of Midland Wagons* (see the Bibliography). This convinced me that the heyday of the steam railway was from about 1890 until the outbreak of the Great War. From my point of view there were a number of advantages in modelling this period, in particular the question of length. Although my layout is an end-to-end affair — a through station with fiddle sidings at each end — the station limits, which include the junction to the goods branch, are between a tunnel mouth and an overbridge and measure almost 40ft. My Edwardian-period

trains do not dominate the scene, but when we placed a model of an LMS 4-6-2 on the line and calculated the length of a 15-coach train I knew that I had made the right decision — a train of that length totally dominated the line. Furthermore, it could not be accommodated in the fiddle yards at either end of the layout beyond the scenic section.

The same principles applied to goods trains: a small 0-6-0 with about a dozen wagons and a goods brake looks very acceptable, but a similar length of train with a Class 8F looks far too short. However, rather than discuss modelling attitudes further, perhaps we should return to the question of the development of passenger trains from the early years of the steam railway and consider how they can be reproduced in model form. In keeping with my perception of the level of interest in the hobby, I have tried to ensure that the pre-1923 period is not over-emphasised.

Chapter One

The Development of Passenger Trains

At the dawn of the railway age, for inland travel the stagecoach was the only means of public transport available, although in making this statement I do recognise that coastal ships and even canal boats were used by some travellers. Stagecoaches will play no part in this book, but they are the natural starting point for our brief historical survey of the development of passenger trains, so it is worth noting that at the dawn of the railway age there were, in 1836, some 3,000 coaches, employing 150,000 horses and 30,000 men. Stagecoaches were advertised to run between particular cities and towns, and usually the starting and terminating point of the journey was an inn. However, the first railways were not built with passenger traffic in mind; the object of the early railways was the movement of goods and minerals, a subject that we will explore in my third book on railway operation for the modeller.

The first 'proper railway' was the Liverpool & Manchester, which opened in 1830. Although this line ran between two major centres of population, the original plans were for but one intermediate station, at Newton Bridge. A further example of the lack of interest in passenger traffic potential by the early railway builders is evident when the original estimate of £2,500,000 for the construction of the London & Birmingham Railway is examined; this did not include any amount for the construction of stations. But this was soon to change, as passenger traffic became an essential part of most British railway companies' sources of revenue.

In his 1898 Presidential Address to the Institution of Mechanical Engineers, S. W. Johnson, Locomotive Superintendent of the Midland Railway, said that from 1862 the growth in passenger numbers had been steady, and he attributed this increase to a number of factors ranging from population increase to lower fares and greater mobility of people whose spending power was increasing. As far as this work is concerned, it means that other than for modellers of purely freight-only lines, some knowledge of the development of passenger train services is useful, if not essential.

JUNE 3, 1898.] ENGINEERING. 705

PASSENGER ROLLING STOCK; MIDLAND RAILWAY.

(See Mr. Johnson's Presidential Address, Page 707.)

Fig 18 — Birmingham & Derby Junc — 1st Class Carriage 1839
Fig. 19. — B. & D. Jn — 2nd Class Carriage 1839
Fig. 20 — Midland Counties Ry — 3rd Class Carriage 1842
Fig. 21 — Midland Counties Ry — 2nd Class Carriage 1844
Fig 22 — Mansfield & Pinxton Ry — 2nd & 3rd Class Compo 1848
Fig 23 — 1st Class Carriage 1848

Fig. 24. — 1st Class Carriage 1848
Fig. 25. — 2nd Class Carriage 1848
Fig. 26 — 3rd Class Carriage (Broad Gauge) 1848
Fig. 27 — 2nd Class Carriage 1858
Fig. 28 — 1st & 2nd Class Compo 1861

Fig. 29 — 3rd Class Carriage, 1865.
Fig. 30 — 1st Class Carriage, 1867.
Fig. 31. — 2nd Class Carriage, 1867.
Fig. 32 — Composite Carriage 1874

Fig. 33 Bogie Composite Carriage, 1875
Fig. 34. Bogie Composite Carriage 1877

Fig. 35. Bogie Composite Carriage, 1889 (Grand Prix Paris)
Fig. 36. 1st Class Dining Carriage, 1896.

Fig. 37. Composite 1st Class Dining Carriage 1897
Fig. 38. 3rd Class Dining Carriage 1897.

In simple terms, passenger trains fall into two main categories, 'Express' and 'Ordinary', although the early timetables usually use the terms Express or Passenger. In addition, most Mail trains also included passenger carriages within the composition of the train. Under the 'Ordinary' passenger train heading we can include branch-line passenger trains, which were locomotive hauled with the engine running round the carriages for the return journey, or, later, 'pull and push' trains, where the locomotive hauled the train in one direction and propelled it in the other. Branch lines also saw the use of 'steam carriages', an LNER term for Sentinel steam railcars, which were also used by the LMS. This class of train was also to be found on the GWR, which operated the greatest number of steam railcars in addition to owning a number of diesel railcars. In conclusion, we must not overlook mixed trains, which catered for both passenger and freight traffic. We will explore the complexities of branch trains later.

The development of traffic dictated improvements in carriage design, and I include some sketches of 19th-century passenger rolling-stock to illustrate how vehicles improved over the years. I do not know of any other source that so neatly encapsulates the changes that took place over a 58-year period. Published in *Engineering* in 1898, it was part of S. W. Johnson's Presidential Address. From this it can be seen that the first carriages ran on four wheels, but six-wheel stock was in service at an early date, and this arrangement of non-bogie stock continued to be built for many years. Indeed, the construction of both four- and six-wheel passenger-carrying stock continued into the 20th century, even though before the end of the 1870s eight-wheel and 12-wheel bogie carriages were in service. However, as John Edgington pointed out when he read the text for this book, the wheel has gone full circle and we are now back to four-wheel stock — those evil Class 142, 143 and 144 DMUs!

Some of the other developments in carriage design up to 1899 and into the 20th century that are not shown in the diagrams include improvements in brakes, the availability of lavatories (at

first with only limited access for passengers), the use of Pullman cars (which began to run in Great Britain in 1876), corridor carriages, dedicated dining and sleeping carriages, and lighting (initially oil, then gas and finally electricity). There is also the question of heating; at first it was non-existent, the first development being foot-warmers, followed by a hot-water system, and finally steam heating supplied from the locomotive. On electrified lines electric heating was used.

The *Engineering* drawing does not show any of the other vehicles that, although they did not carry passengers, also ran in passenger trains and as such were known as 'non-passenger-carrying coaching stock'. Examples of this class of vehicle include passenger brake-vans, mail coaches, parcels, fruit and milk vans, horse-boxes, etc, and we will consider these vehicles in greater detail in Chapter 3.

In my view the classification of passenger trains changed little over the years. I will not complicate matters by discussing in depth the very early arrangements whereby Third Class passengers were not carried on all trains, or the use of 'Parliamentary' trains, which were in effect a daily train, usually starting at an inconvenient hour, in order to comply with the law that compelled the railway companies to run at least one train per day that carried the lowest class of passenger. However, some reference is required for those modellers, albeit few in number, whose models reflect the very early years of the railway system.

The railways classified their passengers by the fares charged and followed stagecoach practice, where the most expensive seats were 'inside' the coach and the cheapest 'outside'. At the beginning of the railway age both First and Second Class passengers travelled in covered vehicles, the difference being the quality of the seating and maybe the arrangement of windows, while Third Class travelled in what was in effect an open wagon. In 1844 an Act of Parliament required that Third Class carriages should have roofs and that at least one train per day should carry Third Class passengers and stop at all stations, but other improvements were slow in coming. These trains were known as 'Parliamentary' or, as some companies described them, 'Government' trains.

The earliest carriages ran on four wheels, and while some readers may consider these vehicles to be rather old-fashioned, they survived in one form or another for many years. The GWR provides one example of the longevity of four-wheel coaches. Writing in *Great Western Coaches from 1890* (see the Bibliography), Michael Harris states that by 1890 the only four-wheel stock being produced by the GWR was for branch-line workings and suburban services, and he gives the figure of 602 as the number of such vehicles built between 1890 and 1902. He continues by saying that by the late 1930s four-wheel stock was restricted to more out-of-the-way branch lines and workmen's trains in South Wales, and concludes by stating that on the Burry Port & Gwendraeth Valley line they

remained in use until 1953, when passenger services were withdrawn. However, there were other sections of railway in Great Britain where four-wheel carriages remained in service for many years, in particular on miners-only trains.

The major change in attitude by the railway companies towards Third Class passengers came in 1875 when the Midland Railway abolished Second Class and upgraded its Third Class to existing Second Class standards, but did not increase Third Class fares. In addition, the company reduced its First Class fares to roughly the old Second Class levels. At about the same time the Midland also admitted Third Class passengers to all trains, which previously had not been common practice. In modern language, it could be seen as a masterstroke of creative marketing, which wrong-footed all the other British railway companies and greatly improved the Midland Railway's image with travellers and its market share of passenger traffic on routes where it competed with other companies. It could also be said that 1875 marked the beginning of the largely two-class system for passenger travel in the United Kingdom, although there were a few routes that retained three classes. David Jenkinson examines this subject in much greater detail in *British Railway Carriages of the 20th Century*, Volume 1 (see the Bibliography), which is recommended reading.

Although many modellers do not worry about reproducing brake blocks on their models, braking systems have an important part to play, if only that the end train pipes should show the type of brakes fitted. In the United Kingdom the preferred braking system for the majority of railway companies, once the various trials had taken place and it became a legal requirement to have a proper braking system, was the 'Vacuum Automatic', but some companies used the Westinghouse system. The use of two non-compatible systems meant there was a need for some companies to have both locomotives and stock that were dual-fitted — see the accompanying extract from the 1922 *Railway Year Book*, which shows the position at the time of the Grouping. In the years that followed, both locomotives and rolling-stock were converted from Westinghouse to the automatic vacuum, and modellers should be aware of which line used which system if this is to be accurately portrayed on their models.

Before considering the developments that took place after the end of the century, I would like briefly to draw readers' attention to what I see as the importance of the 1890s in the history of British railway development. The steam railway proper spanned the period from the opening of the Liverpool & Manchester in 1830 until steam ceased to be used on British main-line railways in 1968, a period of 138 years. Therefore the halfway mark would be 1899, and that was indeed a pivotal point and a time when considerable changes were taking place. These largely stemmed from the concept of providing improved amenities for passengers, for example gangways between coaches, to enable them to move from coach to coach, increased lavatory

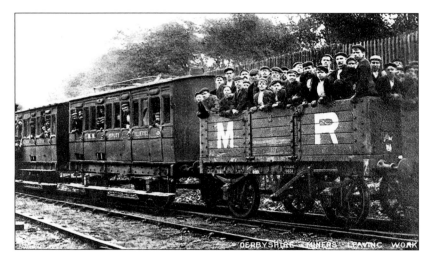

Left: The carriages of this miners' train appear to be the 1865 Third Class carriages shown as Fig 29 in the 1898 *Engineering* drawings, and the nearest is lettered 'Ripley Collieries'. The condition of the track suggests that this is part of the colliery sidings and that the train will take the miners only a short distance. The date is probably between 1900 and 1914, and although early passenger trains carried Third Class passengers in open trucks, well before this picture was taken such practices were no longer allowed on main lines, but only on private sidings. *Author's collection*

Below left: This is one of the earliest pictures known to me that shows a branch-line passenger train of the 19th century, in this case at the terminus of the Midland Railway's Dursley branch in Gloucestershire, opened in 1856. It is not easy to date, but the late David Tee, in my view the most knowledgeable of all Midland Railway historians, said that it might be between 1866 and 1875, and although it has been published before, I felt that it should be included to illustrate what some passenger trains were like circa 1870. There are no automatic brakes — they are still years away for this class of train — and just two small oil-lit four-wheel carriages. *Author's collection*

Below: Although most modellers seem to prefer the post-1948 era, it is not possible to ignore the early years if, as modellers, we want to show all aspects of our railway history; indeed, the background buildings do look rather like models! S&DJR No 17 was built by George England in 1865 and later rebuilt at Derby as seen here, at Burnham. The probable date is circa 1885, but it is difficult to date the carriages. They are similar to the 1858/61 vehicles seen in the *Engineering* drawings; for example, the coach at the far end of the train retains the luggage rack on the roof, while the leading coach appears to have a brake compartment — at least the louvres for a dog box can be seen. At this date some of the lesser British railways were somewhat primitive; note the flat-bottom track and general uncared-for appearance, which was not typical of this period on the leading British railway companies. *Author's collection*

Railway Year Book.

AUTOMATIC BRAKE SYSTEMS OF THE UNITED KINGDOM.

Westinghouse Automatic.

Standard for steam trains on the following railways : Caledonian, Castlederg and Victoria Bridge, Colne Valley and Halstead, Glasgow District Subway (Cable), Great Eastern, Great North of Scotland, Isle of Wight, Isle of Wight Central, Listowel and Ballybunion, London, Brighton and South Coast, Midland (London, Tilbury and Southend Section), Mid-Suffolk Light, North British (vacuum is being adopted), North Eastern, North Wales Narrow Gauge, Rhymney, South Eastern and Chatham (L. C. & D. Section), Stratford-upon-Avon and Midland Junction. Also on engines taken over from the Government for heavy goods service.

Used for electric trains as follows : Central London, City and South London, Great Western and Metropolitan Joint Stock, London and North Western and North London, London and South Western, London Electric, Liverpool Overhead, Mersey, Metropolitan, Metropolitan District.

Vacuum Automatic.

Standard for steam trains on the following railways : Ballinascarthy, Barry, Belfast and County Down, Bideford, Westward Ho! and Appledore, Brecon and Merthyr, Cambrian, Cavan and Leitrim, Cheshire Lines, Clogher Valley, Corris, Cork, Bandon, and South Coast, Cork, Blackrock, and Passage, Cork and Macroom Direct, Cork and Muskerry, County Donegal Joint, Dublin and South Eastern, Dundalk, Newry, and Greenore, Festiniog, Furness, Glasgow and South Western, Great Central, Great Northern (England), Great Northern (Ireland), Great Southern and Western, Great Western, Highland, Hull and Barnsley, Knott End, Lambourn Valley, Lancashire and Yorkshire (steam and electric), London and North Western (steam trains), London and South Western (steam trains), Londonderry and Lough Swilly, Maryport and Carlisle, Metropolitan (steam trains), Midland, Midland (Northern Counties Committee, Ireland), Midland and Great Northern Joint, Midland Great Western, Midland and South Western Junction, Neath and Brecon, North London, North Staffordshire, Portpatrick and Wigtownshire, Rhondda and Swansea Bay, Sligo, Leitrim and Northern Counties, Somerset and Dorset Joint, South Eastern and Chatham (S. E. Section), Taff Vale, Timoleague and Courtmacsherry, Tralee and Dingle, West and South Clare, Wirral.

Dual Fitted.

For working through trains dual fittings are provided on vehicles operating joint services, of which the following may be mentioned : West Coast Joint Stock, East Coast Joint Stock, Midland-North British Joint Stock, London and North Western-North Eastern services, and certain other through facilities. Many railways have a number of engines fitted for working trains having the other of the two standard brake equipments.

Left: An extract from the 1922 *Railway Year Book* listing the braking systems used by British railway companies at the time of the Grouping.

Below: This picture has been included to show a North Eastern Railway horsebox that is dual-fitted. The taller vacuum pipe — or, to use the correct term, 'end train pipe' — is for the automatic vacuum brake, the other is for the Westinghouse brake. Vehicles that were dual-fitted also carried the necessary equipment to work either system, and this can be seen between the solebars. Note that the brake hand lever is at the left-hand end of the vehicle, rather than at the right, which was a more usual arrangement for hand brakes. *Author's collection*

Left: I have mentioned heating systems and the need to include the necessary equipment. The first passenger carriages did not have any form of heating; then foot-warmers, a primitive form of hot-water bottle, became available. Matters improved when a hot-water system began to be installed, but during the early years of the 20th century steam heating became the established method of heating passenger carriages. Regardless of the outside temperature, there were clearly defined dates when carriage heating had to be applied, known as the 'carriage warming season' or something similar — the precise wording varied between the different companies. From the modelling standpoint, modellers can dispense with all steam heating pipes and assume that it is the height of summer, or, if they wish to portray a model that depicts the period between, say, October and April, then steam heating pipes are required. Pictures that show steam heating are commonplace, but pictures of the hot-water system are not. Therefore I have included this picture of Midland 0-4-4T No 1533, taken at Manchester Central some time between 1892, when it was fitted with a hot-water system, and 1900, when the locomotive received a new boiler. *Author's collection*

Below left: On many model railways the combination of over-sharp curves and out-of-scale automatic couplings makes it almost impossible to achieve the correct coupling of corridor carriages. Note that the gangway connections are together, with no gap between them, and that the faces of the buffers are touching. The screw coupling does not have any slack and the vacuum hoses are connected. The absence of the steam heating pipes suggests that when this picture of two Midland square-light clerestory coaches was taken it was not during the steam heating season. *Author's collection*

accommodation, dining and sleeping cars, and improved heating and lighting, etc. All these improvements greatly increased the tare weight per passenger that the locomotives had to haul, and this meant that for the same number of passengers the weight of the train increased considerably. There was also a need to increase the overall speed of the trains, which meant that what was 'state of the art' in 1890 was outdated 10 or so years later. When compared with the new vehicles being built for main-line trains in 1890, there had been an immense overall improvement by the early years of the next century. Although passengers would have been conscious of these improvements, the greatest amount of publicity by the railway press and attention by railway enthusiasts of the day would have been paid to the new, more powerful designs of locomotives that were required to haul these heavier trains. We will examine this in greater detail when we consider the types of locomotives used to haul passenger trains in Chapter 4.

One aspect of passenger trains that is not, as far as I am aware, reproduced today on model railways is the practice of slipping coaches; this is understandable, as it is not easy to accomplish.

Above: A view of the Up platform of Marthwaite station with an ex-LNWR railmotor, one of six that were built in two batches, standing at the platform. This unit was used on the Kendal Castle to Marthwaite service and, as part of the working timetable for the line, it also ran to Arnside via the Hincaster branch. On some workings it was diagrammed to work a non-passenger-carrying coaching stock vehicle, see page 33. Note that the platform seats have the station name on the backrest and there are two different pieces of equipment to move parcels on view. *Tony Wright*

Right: Pictures of carriages being slipped are rare, but I do have this example that shows a Midland Railway Brake Composite Lavatory carriage being slipped, location and date unknown. This vehicle had a brake compartment at each end with two First and three Third Class compartments; there were separate lavatories for each class of passenger in the centre of the train. Note the observation window in the end of the coach. I have seen a coach slipped on a model railway; it was on a Great Western model, and the effect was very good indeed. *Author's collection*

According to C. E. J. Fryer's *A History of Slipping and Slip Carriages* (see the Bibliography) the practice of slipping coaches may have started in 1858 on the South Eastern Railway, and continued to develop during the years that followed. The years between 1901 and 1914 may be seen as the peak of the 'slipping era', but thereafter the practice went into rapid decline, and it was almost discontinued during the Great War. During the early years of the Grouping period there was a resurgence of interest, but it was largely to be found on the GWR. In 1928 there were 40 weekday slips on the GWR, none on the LMS, four on the LNER, and only two on the Southern Railway, a fall from the 31 slips that had been the daily total during 1924. The use of slips continued on British Railways, but only on the Western Region, until it finally came to an end in 1960.

However, when compiling *British Railway Modelling Special: Classic Layouts* I used the practice of slipping coaches on models as a way of pointing out to readers that, when compared with what can be obtained today, the models of yesteryear were extremely crude; then in 1909 there was an article in *Models, Railways and Locomotives* that explained how slipping coaches could be reproduced in model form. At some future exhibition I look forward to seeing the practice of slipping coaches on a model railway; the technology to make it work certainly exists, as does the information.

It would probably be true to say that during the 1890s the major changes in respect of improved passenger amenities got under way, but within 10 or so years the railway companies' attention began to be directed towards cost savings on lightly used services and the effect of competition from tramway systems in the more heavily populated areas. The latter led to the first steps towards electrification. Although this series of books is directed towards steam railway modellers, we cannot entirely exclude other forms of traction. As tramway systems developed in major centres of population they became a source of competition to the railways, while the ever-increasing costs of operation on what were essentially country branches or lines

that did not generate high levels of revenue gave cause for concern to senior railway managers. It is not within my terms of reference to consider the underground lines that had links with the main-line railways — I examined that subject as far as the LT&SR was concerned in my book on that company (see the Bibliography) — or the first electrification schemes to come into service, but they do provide modelling opportunities that some may wish to consider. A useful source of further information about this will be found in David Jenkinson's above mentioned work.

In order to combat the increasing costs of operation in such rural areas or those threatened by tramway competition, which was reducing the revenue from short-distance passenger traffic, the railway companies introduced a variety of ideas ranging from petrol-engined railcars and steam railcars to the use of a conventional steam engine that could work a train without the need to run round the stock at the end of each journey. It is this concept that has found considerable favour with modellers, and branch lines operated by this class of train are frequently the

Rail-Motor-Car crossing
Pwllywrach Viaduct. Gwaun-Cae-Gurwen.
— D. Jenkins & Sons — Photo. —

Left: This delightful picture could be a model, but in fact shows a GWR railmotor crossing a viaduct on one of the company's lines in South Wales. Railmotors were introduced during the early 1900s in an attempt to reduce the cost of operating lines where good revenue could not be achieved. Many modellers do not have enough space to build main-line stations, so a branch line becomes an attractive alternative, perhaps with railmotors similar to the one seen here. *Author's collection*

Below left: Although this book is directed towards the steam railway modeller, I felt that I ought to include this 1956 picture, taken on the Liverpool Overhead Railway at Aintree Sefton Arms, to show an example of what could be described as an 'inner city electrified line that could compete with road transport'. *Collection of the late D. F. Tee*

Bottom left: This picture of 0-6-0T No 228, taken at Worthing in 1930, is included to represent a motor train, with the locomotive between the carriages, although an alternative arrangement was for it to be attached at one end. The operating difference was that when the engine was between the carriages the driver was always in one of the driving compartments at each end, but when it was at one end the driver would be on the locomotive if it was pulling or in the driving compartment if it was pushing. Note the rather relaxed approach taken by the fireman while filling the locomotive's side tanks. *J. A. G. H. Coltas*

Right: Steam railmotors entered service from the early 1900s, but this LNER Sentinel was not built until 1929. The LNER was a major user of these units and obtained 80 similar vehicles between 1925 and 1932. They were designed to reduce operating costs and combat competition from road transport. No 39 *Protector* remained in service until 1944, and the type was extinct by 1948. The LMS was also a user of Sentinel steam railmotors, but not to the same extent as the LNER. They offer modellers of branch lines an alternative to a steam locomotive hauling one or two coaches.
Author's collection

Below right: This overhead view was taken at Marthwaite looking in the Down direction towards the tunnel, with the lay bye and the connection to the quarry on the left. This is one of David's 'Funny Trains', in this case a model of the Glasgow and Aberdeen portion of the 1908 West Coast Joint Stock 2pm 'Corridor'. The train was hauled by a model of an LNWR 'George the Fifth' class 4-4-0, No 1595 *Wild Duck*, which was another of his jokes — the most well-known species of wild duck is a Mallard. In the Down direction the train was divided north of the border, but in the Up direction it ran as a complete train. Running at a scale 60mph, this train, with his magnificent 12-wheel carriages, was a splendid sight and one to be savoured.
Tony Wright

subjects of models. Although very little appears to have been written about the actual work entailed with operating what were known as 'motor trains', readers interested in this subject may find Jim Jackson's article, listed in the Bibliography, of value.

It would probably be true to say that after the improvements of circa 1900 were in place, many of the developments that followed were of a comparatively minor nature, and it was only after the 1923 Grouping that the stimulus for further change began to take effect. One factor was that, following the Great War, there was an immense backlog of repairs and renewals to be dealt with, and for a few years from 1923 there was a major programme of new work undertaken by the 'Big Four' railway companies to improve matters. However, the problems of the 1920s were immense; a major downturn in trade and cut-throat competition from road transport caused the railways to reduce costs wherever they could, and this can be reflected in models of the period, even if it is only the introduction

of motor trains on branch-line services, although within this context we should not overlook the various self-propelled vehicles, using different means of propulsion. Because the majority of modellers are interested in the Grouping era and later, however, we will consider the arrangements that applied then in greater detail than those before 1923.

The 1930s marked the introduction of streamlining on both the LMS and the LNER, which was associated with the luxury trains of the era. While this work is about railway operation rather than a detailed history of the development of trains, it is worth noting that luxury and streamlining are not synonymous. The height of luxury probably came with Pullman carriages, where meals and drinks were served in dining cars where the passenger sat throughout the journey. But streamlining provided a degree of excitement, which came as a welcome relief as the years of depression of the late 1920s gave way to a feeling that things were improving. Sadly this was not to last, and

Top left: There can be little doubt that a streamlined locomotive with its rake of carriages presented an impressive sight, and I recall seeing them when my younger brother and I went trainspotting at Tamworth during the early 1940s. To represent these trains I have included this picture of one of the first five to be built by the LMS, No 6222 *Queen Mary,* photographed near Rugby in 1938. *J. A. G. H. Coltas*

Above left: Notwithstanding the glamour of the streamlined trains, the height of luxury for rail travel was the Pullman car, and here is the Up 'Harrogate Pullman' hauled by Great Central Railway 4-6-0 No 1165 *Valour* at about the time of the Grouping — in my view it makes a magnificent sight. The locomotive was built in 1920 and withdrawn in December 1947. *Author's collection*

Left: I used an LMS train to represent the streamliners, and this picture of LNER Gresley 4-6-2 No 4475 provides an example of a named main-line express train. The locomotive is in immaculate condition, and I have always felt that the teak-coloured carriages went well with the apple-green livery used by the LNER at that time. *Author's collection*

Top: Rather than use an 'ordinary' picture to show an 'Ordinary' passenger train on a cross-country working, I thought readers might be interested to see the combination that they could use if they modelled a joint line, in this case the Shrewsbury & Hereford, GWR & LNWR Joint, during the Grouping period. This picture was taken circa 1936 at Craven Arms and shows ex-LNWR 4-6-0 No 25751 from Shrewsbury shed at the head of a Shrewsbury to Hereford

passenger train. What makes this picture so interesting is that the locomotive is owned by the LMS and the coaches by the GWR. On page 23 I have given examples of other trains that used the stock of both companies on alternate days; this practice was commonplace on some joint lines and could provide the modeller with an opportunity to run some interesting trains. *Lens of Sutton*

Above: One of the most intensively worked lines for 'residential' traffic was the London, Tilbury & Southend Railway, which became the LT&S Section of the Midland Division of the LMS. This 1936 picture shows 4-4-2T No 2136 on a Fenchurch Street to Southend passenger train at Leigh-on-Sea. The 11-coach set is made up of LMS non-corridor stock. *Courtesy of John Jennison*

Right: I thought it would be interesting to show that through coaches were not confined to main-line express trains. This 1910 picture shows an unidentified LNWR 2-4-2T working the 9.55am Leicester to Nuneaton passenger train passing below the Great Central line near Narborough and Whetstone. The through coach is a Midland Railway vehicle, almost certainly a Brake Composite coupled behind the engine and being worked from Nottingham to Leamington Spa. *G. M. Shoults*

Above: Inspection Saloons were used by railway company directors and engineers to inspect sections of the line. They could be pulled or propelled, but when an inspection was taking place it was normal practice to run with the coach leading, the uninterrupted view from the end enabling a thorough inspection to take place. The motive power used for this work varied, but a small passenger engine was most suitable. This picture of ex-Midland Railway 4-4-0 No 534 was taken at Berkhamsted on 7 May 1948. *H. C. Casserley*

the life of the high-speed streamlined steam trains was short — World War 2 saw to that. The most comprehensive story of these trains will be found in A. J. Mullay's book listed in the Bibliography, while details of the stock used in these trains are given in the various other titles listed there. There can be little doubt that the spectacle of streamlined trains running at speed would have been very impressive, and they provided a wonderful advertising and promotional opportunity for the railway companies; indeed, it is recorded that on the LNER they were rather profitable, but we should not forget that they represented but a minute fraction of the daily passenger train working mileage for each company. Nevertheless, they provide a very popular prototype for modellers, but we should perhaps return to rather more mundane matters.

There were three kinds of train services that conveyed passengers. Main-line 'Express' trains were run at high speeds, generally over long distances with no or few intermediate stops. Their purpose was to serve important towns and cities between which there was an established need for both rapid and regular communication. The most prestigious of these trains were named, probably the most famous being the 'Flying Scotsman', although this statement could be open to debate!

The next category was what the LMS referred to as 'general purpose'. The company, in one of its internal documents, said that some might be described as long-distance main-line fast and stopping trains, while others provided cross-country connections. Local services were also included in this category.

Finally, the LMS regarded the trains that ran between large cities and their suburban areas as being a separate and third category of passenger train, sometimes using the term 'residential' to describe them.

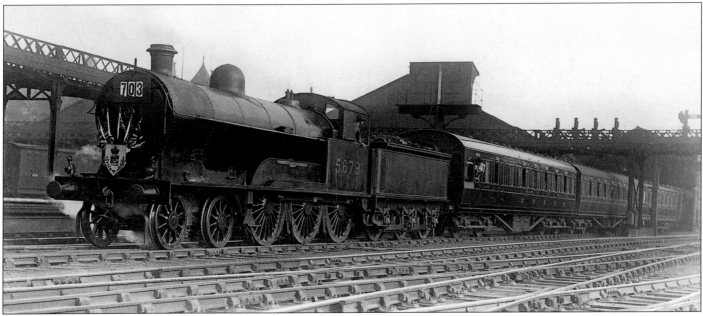

Although I will consider 'through' coaches in greater depth in the next chapter, they need to be mentioned here. Rarely does one see a through coach attached or detached on a model railway, and in my view this is probably because they do not feature on the modern railway, and as a result they are overlooked as an operating feature. Briefly, a through coach enabled passengers to remain in the same vehicle throughout the journey, during which it would be detached from one train and attached to another as route changes dictated. It was a very civilised way to travel.

Within this chapter we should also consider the traffic that was generated by what was known as 'cheap fares', and within this category I will also consider what could be described as 'passenger-carrying non-scheduled trains'. Although the LMS document referred to above does not specifically include excursion trains within the 'general purpose' category, this is

Top: Excursion trains provided the railway companies with large numbers of passengers, in particular during the summer months, when many of the northern towns went on holiday during the same week of the year. This picture was taken near Preston during the late 1920s and shows a typical excursion train of the era. The carriages are a mixture of Midland, LNWR and L&YR, with at least three still in their pre-Grouping liveries. At times of peak travel it was normal practice to cancel many freight trains, providing the required paths for the excursion trains and also releasing both locomotives and train crews to work them. As long as the driver and guard signed for the route, the services would be worked by men who would normally only work freight trains. If they did not sign, they could be provided with a pilotman who did sign. Furthermore, it was commonplace to use 0-6-0 goods engines to work these trains. *Author's collection*

Above: It was not unusual for excursion trains to carry special headboards in addition to the reporting number that was required for operating purposes. This picture of ex-LNWR 4-6-0 'Prince of Wales' No 5679 was taken at Crewe when the locomotive was working a Boy Scout special train. In addition to the reporting number 703 at the top of the smokebox, the Boy Scouts' flags and badge have been attached to the centre front lamp holder. This would have been custom-made, whereas close examination of the print clearly shows that the reporting number has been made up using a board to which separate numbers could be applied; these boards were prepared at the engine shed that provided the motive power for the train. *Author's collection*

17

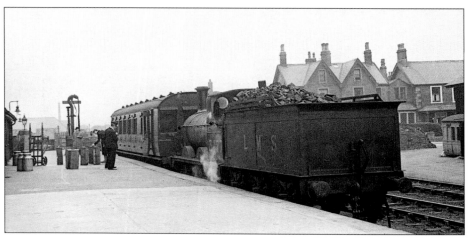

Left: LNER 'B7' class 4-6-0 No 1365, working an express passenger train at Retford in 1947, has either just taken water or is about to — it is not clear whether the fireman is pulling the water crane arm into position or has thrown the chain to the driver so that he can pull it clear. I suspect the former, and the driver is moving towards the water valve to turn it on. Note the frost fire and the accumulated ash behind the ground disc signal. *Author's collection*

Below left: Passenger train services on branch lines often provide modellers with the opportunity to use a variety of locomotives. This picture, taken at Barnoldswick on 11 June 1947, illustrates what is possible. The coach is a Motor Driving Trailer and the train has just arrived at the station — but it is not a motor train. The locomotive is a Johnson Class 2F 0-6-0, a type that was sometimes used to work branch-line passenger trains during Midland, LMS and even early British Railways days, but they were not motor-fitted. I presume that for some reason a motor-fitted engine was not available, which is why the Class 2 is working the train. This picture is also useful in showing milk churns and other passenger-rated traffic that will be loaded into the brake compartment of the coach. *H. C. Casserley*

Right: This overhead view of Marthwaite shows No 5902 *Sir Frank Ree*, one of two 'Claughtons' that were rebuilt in 1930 and were later known as 'Patriots'. This picture is full of modelling interest. Note the barrow crossing connecting both platforms and the warning notice boards, the water crane and tall starting signal close to the elevated water tank. In the distance we can see cottages and road vehicles. Even though they do not move, the presence of people adds life to the picture. *Tony Wright*

where they were placed. Recently I asked my local station how many different fares there were for a journey between Derby and London, and I was amazed to discover how many variations were available. The difference between railways today and before World War 2 is that today generally the same stock is used — it is only the price that varies — but during the steam railway era the rolling-stock could also vary with the price of the ticket.

From a modelling point of view, we can consider how this 'cheap fare' traffic can be reproduced, and there are several options — a works outing, for example. It was not uncommon for large companies to run a number of special trains for their employees' annual outings, and reproducing a special event of this nature would undoubtedly stretch the resources of most, if not all, model railways. To the best of my knowledge this is a topic that, with one exception, has never been the subject of a book. The exception is Rod Pearson's *The Bass Railway Trips* (see the Bibliography), and readers may find this work to be of great interest. It records that the first Bass trip was from Burton to Liverpool on 19 August 1865, when about 1,000 people were taken in two trains. Although the last organised Bass trip

from Burton-on-Trent was in 1924, it was the only one to run after the Great War and went to the British Empire Exhibition in London. The number of trains run on each trip to a seaside destination during the period 1900–14 was between 14 and 17, and the number of passengers carried often exceeded 10,000. Although the changed conditions that applied after the Great War caused Bass to cease running their special trains, other companies continued the practice, albeit on a greatly reduced scale, and it represents an interesting modelling opportunity, if only by the addition of a headboard and perhaps a slight alteration to the composition of a train.

Smaller parties of 'cheap fare' travellers could have a coach set aside for their needs, which could be attached to one train, then detached and coupled to a second train to enable the party to reach their destination. These moves, either attaching or detaching, could be reproduced on many layouts. Over the years I have watched many model railways, but the practice of shunting coaches only infrequently takes place.

Within the single-coach category we must not overlook Picnic Saloons and Invalid Saloons — both were in regular use — and there was also the Railway Officers or Directors Saloon, which

is rarely reproduced in model form. If you believe that model railways should err on the side of maximum activity, then the incorporation of marshalling carriages by moving them from one train to another is one way of increasing visual interest, but only if the track layout and signals permit these moves to be carried out in a realistic way.

In my view the introduction of the various types of excursion train offers modellers the greatest opportunity for the creative modelling of passenger trains. An excursion was considered to be a journey for health or pleasure, and the first was organised by Thomas Cook and run between Leicester and Loughborough in 1841. As they became established, they could usually be divided into one of two categories: the guaranteed excursion, which was usually a special train run solely for a particular party, and the advertised excursion by special train, for which members of the public could purchase tickets. Another form of excursion was the arrangement whereby bookings were open to the public at excursion fares and they could travel on certain trains included in scheduled train services. All these options have modelling opportunities.

From a modelling standpoint both the guaranteed and advertised excursions require a set of carriages, which could vary from an aged set that was used only a few times each year, to coaches that were in regular use but were taken from their normal services and used for the excursion traffic. For example, non-corridor stock used on 'residential' services could be used on excursion services during a Bank Holiday. It was usual practice for these trains to carry 'reporting numbers' on the locomotive, often together with an identifying headboard. This practice also applied to trains hired by single parties, for example company or works outings, where usually the locomotive carried a distinctive headboard that was made for that particular occasion. I have also seen pictures that show a form of reporting number on the end of the last coach in the train; I do not know how common this practice was, but I believe that it would apply only to special trains that ran in more than one part, a practice described as 'duplicated'.

At first sight there appears to be no modelling opportunity for an excursion that was in effect passengers with cheap tickets travelling on a scheduled train service, but this would be wrong. It was not uncommon to have to 'strengthen' trains at major stations in order to accommodate additional passengers, and this again provides the opportunity to add one or more coaches to the train. The train would arrive at the platform, the train engine would uncouple and draw forward 'out of the way' and another engine would set back onto the train with the extra coach(es). An alternative would be for the train engine to uncouple and pick up the additional coach(es) before setting back onto the train. A further option would be to add the strengthening vehicles to the rear of the train by using a pilot engine while the train engine remained coupled at the front.

The need for the train engine to take water should also not be overlooked, and this could be a factor in deciding which method of attaching the coaches to use. For example, if the train engine was uncoupled from the train it could stand by a water column while the pilot engine set the coaches back onto the train, but if the vehicles were to be added from the rear of the train then water could be taken at the platform where the train had stopped. It is these touches that separate a realistic model, which shows how the steam railway was operated, from those

where the operators have less idea of how things were done.

Before the Great War the level of Sunday excursion traffic was quite low, but from the 1920s onwards there was an enormous increase and it was not unusual for excursion trains to be seen on branch lines that, during the week, would never see more than a two- or three-coach set, while a Sunday excursion might be a nine- or ten-coach train. Therefore modellers of branch lines could introduce Sunday specials with 'interesting' trains to confound some viewers.

To summarise, the scope for creative modelling by the use of excursion and special trains is considerable: Bank Holiday excursions, race trains, football specials, Army, Navy and Air Force movements, agricultural shows, circus trains, theatrical traffic and special trains run in connection with steamer services. Furthermore, some of these trains would be made up by using modern stock, and the use of dining cars on many of these services was far from unknown. An example was the all-Pullman excursion train 'Eastern Belle', which was introduced in 1929 from London Liverpool Street to a different destination each week.

Age of Carriage Stock

To conclude this chapter I have selected an illustration that shows part of an ex-Midland Railway set of non-corridor carriages. There is nothing particularly unusual about the carriage, a Third Brake Compartment vehicle, or indeed the one coupled to it, another ex-Midland vehicle from the same era. My reason for including this picture is simply to draw attention to the question of age. The date of the picture is given as circa 1956, and I would not disagree — clearly it was after the rebuilding of Birmingham New Street station, where it was taken.

In my discussions with modellers, who are only interested in the period of railway history they can remember, I have tried to point out that in the 1950s there was still a large amount of pre-Grouping stock running, and to concentrate only on Stanier and later-period stock for their models is quite wrong. Unfortunately, many believe they only saw the more modern vehicles during that period, and as a result their models lack elderly stock, which also applies to locomotives and wagons. During the years that followed Nationalisation there was an immense backlog of repairs and renewals to overcome, and I would guess that the average age of carriages in 1948 was well in excess of 20 years, which means that many carriages still in service were 40 or more years old. I have no details of the average age of LMS carriages beyond an estimate made just prior to World War 2, giving the expected position as at 31 December 1940, which

supports the view expressed above. I doubt if these figures would be very different if applied to the other 'Big Four' companies. The figures given are the estimated average ages for classes of carriage stock:

Restaurant vehicles	13.82 years
Steam-hauled stock, First Class	15.86 years
Third Class	14.88 years
Composites	16.14 years
Average of total for steam-hauled stock	15.21 years
Electric-hauled stock	13.03 years
Sleeping cars	15.16 years
Non-passenger-carrying vehicles	17.05 years

The projection given in the Traffic Committee minutes, which is the source of this information, said that for renewal purposes the LMS should assume an average life of sleeping, restaurant and kitchen cars of 30 years, other passenger-carrying stock 38 years, horseboxes and fish vans 30 years, and all other non-passenger-carrying stock 38 years. As I have said, World War 2 increased the average age of stock, and a modeller who wishes to give an accurate picture of the post-war steam railway should bear these figures in mind. *Photo D. Ibbotson*

The named express trains were composed of the most modern corridor stock, and generally the railway companies followed the principle of 'cascading down', with the latest vehicles being used on the best trains and the carriages they superseded replacing older stock on less important trains and so on, with the very oldest stock being relegated to occasional excursion use before being scrapped. It was

not always quite so neat and tidy, but this was the principle used. The named trains included dining cars, often running with separate kitchen cars, and sleeping carriages when appropriate.

During the period from the 1923 Grouping to World War 2, the major improvements to passenger rolling-stock were driven by the need to compete with road transport, in par-

ticular the motor coach. These improvements included the use of shoulder lights and arm rests in Third Class carriages, deep-waisted windows, more modern upholstery, woodwork, and improved ventilation and heating. First Class sleeping cars were often upgraded, and Third Class sleeping cars introduced for passengers who could not afford to travel First Class. At first they had four berths with rugs

and pillows; two-berth Third Class sleeping carriages did not appear until after World War 2 on the LNER and LMS.

By the 1930s the typical length of carriages being introduced or in use on main-line trains was generally between 57 and 60ft, although some were longer — 65ft or slightly more was not unusual. Non-corridor stock was generally between 50 and 57ft, but it should be remembered that these are typical lengths and there were many pre-Grouping vehicles in service at this time and even well into the British Railways era, and these were often shorter in length. In the Bibliography I have listed a number of books that describe the coaching stock of various railway companies, and I recommend that readers refer to them for more precise details of the coaching stock used on their preferred lines.

The composition of the most important of the 'general purpose' trains was not very inferior to that of the named trains, but those considered less important by the railway companies would have older vehicles and perhaps non-corridor stock. The make-up of branch trains varied, and often the factor determining the type of vehicle used was the distance covered; some trains were made up of corridor

stock, while others had non-corridor vehicles and, when used on cross-country routes, the provision of lavatory accommodation has to be taken into account. For suburban or 'residential' trains the essential feature was stock that would allow the maximum number of passengers to be carried. These trains were generally made up by using non-corridor non-lavatory carriages, although the use of semi-vestibule stock was not uncommon. The carriages used with motor trains and railcars were adapted for this purpose; some were purpose-built, while others were conversions from existing stock.

While generally the stock of the constituent companies of the 'Big Four' remained on its home ground, some transfers did take place. An example of inter-divisional transfers during the early years of the LMS was the movement of ex-Midland Railway carriages from the Midland Division of the LMS to the Highland Section of the Northern Division. This was to improve the quality of stock available for normal services. Another transfer was the displacement of ex-North London Railway stock to South Wales, and I have no doubt that similar transfers applied to all the 'Big Four' companies during the post-1923 era and into the BR period.

Above: The first hundred Horwich Moguls were painted in Crimson Lake so naturally David's model was one of this batch in the original livery; naturally I fully approved of his choice. This picture shows No 13004 at the head of the 'Dalesman' about to enter Kendal Castle station. He built the magnificent model of the Period 1 Corridor Brake Composite at the head of the train and, like all of his carriages, it is rather splendid. *Tony Wright*

Chapter Two

Train Formation, Vehicles and Working Practice

Although the 1898 extract from *Engineering* in Chapter 1 gives a reasonable idea of the development of passenger rolling-stock during the 19th century, very little has survived about the formation of trains during the early years of the steam railway. There are reports of excursion trains made up of 20 or more carriages hauled by more than one engine, but of course no photographic evidence exists, this early period pre-dating the camera. There are some early engravings, but their accuracy is questionable.

Early passenger trains were made up of a mixture of carriages that catered for First and Second Class passengers only, with at least one train per day over every line conveying Third Class passengers, which stopped at all stations; I assume that these trains also had provision for the other classes. Later, Third Class passengers could travel by all trains. In the years before the automatic brake became a legal requirement for all passenger trains, separate brake vehicles were included within the composition of the train, each vehicle carrying a brakeman who responded to the driver's instructions given by the engine's whistle. It was all very primitive by the standards that had become universal practice by the final decade of the 19th century.

A recent article by Jack Braithwaite in *Midland Record* (see the Bibliography) puts the very important Midland Railway London to Nottingham 'Scotch' trains into perspective, and in some respects the diagram reproduced in the article may be considered as being representative of British railway express train development during the 1890s. It shows that over this far from easy route a mean speed of 52mph applied to both trains, but the train weight of the 10.35am in 1890, which became the 10.40am in 1900, had increased from 111 to 186 tons.

Passenger Station Working, published by the LMS School of Transport in 1938, contains a statement in the section dealing with platforming that intrigued me; the comments are particularly valid for modellers, so I reproduce them in full:

'The governing principle in station platforming is the time factor, and this resolves itself into the question of making the best use of the facilities available to complete the station work with a passenger train in the minimum space of time.

Many of the problems which present themselves are the direct result of inadequate facilities to deal with present-day traffic as present-day standards dictate. This can be illustrated by the demands made on a station loading 700 long-distance excursion passengers. In 1920 these could have been accommodated in 15 six-wheeled carriages, occupying 510ft of platform length, but under present-day conditions, accommodated in vestibule stock, the same number of passengers would require 13 bogie vehicles, occupying 788ft of platform length. Should dining facilities be given for the same number of passengers, two trains with a total of 18 vehicles, occupying 1,060ft of platform length, would be required. Thus, under present-day standards, over twice the length of platform per passenger is required to deal with the same number of passengers as a few years ago.'

What this internal LMS document is saying is that the facilities that were satisfactory before 1920 are no longer adequate in 1938, and although it is an LMS training manual, the point it makes would also apply to the other British railway companies. From a modeller's standpoint there are two lessons: first, it is not incorrect to have cramped station facilities that are awkward to operate; and second, modelling an earlier period makes better use of the limited space that most of us have available, a point that I have made earlier, but which cannot be overstated if we are to make the best use of the space we have for our model railways.

The composition of a railway company's principal express trains was shown in the relevant 'Marshalling Book' or 'Marshalling Circular'. These marshalling diagrams contained a variety of information:

* The order in the train that the vehicles were assembled
* The seating capacity of each vehicle

Below and below right: Both these are examples of long-distance parcels trains on the Western Division taken from the 4 July 1938 Marshalling Book. Note the designated traffic in the vans from Birmingham that were transferred at Crewe. The marshalling and re-marshalling of both trains was typical of the way parcels trains made their way across the railway system, and should provide food for thought for owners of main-line layouts.

Marshalling Arrangements and Circuit Diagrams

In *Railway Operation for the Modeller* I included a number of examples of passenger train marshalling, taken from the LMS Marshalling Arrangements for 9 July 1934, and all describing trains on the company's Midland Division. For this book I have widened the selection to include examples from other LMS divisions, but all are typical of marshalling arrangements that applied elsewhere in the country.

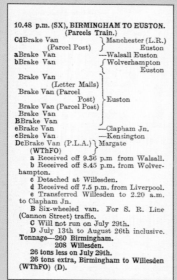

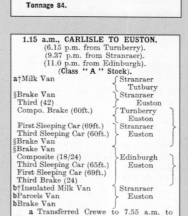

Left: This simple example, taken from the June 1938 LMS Northern Division book, shows that not all marshalling arrangements were complex. The three coaches from Kyle were combined with others at Inverness to form a train to Perth.

Left: This is a fascinating example of an overnight train, taken from the 4 July 1938 Western Division Marshalling Book, and shows a train that conveyed Scottish traffic to London. The Tutbury milk van would be attached to a train for Stoke, then to another train to be worked forward to Tutbury, probably on a Stoke to Derby service. Note there were arrangements for two separate sleeping sections, one for passengers from Larne in Ireland via the ferry to Stranraer, and the other from Edinburgh.

* The destination of each vehicle
* The previous working of the stock to the station responsible for marshalling the train
* The weight of each train, to enable the provision of the correct type of engine

Examples of LMS carriage marshalling arrangements for passenger trains are reproduced here.

The information also appeared in the 'Carriage Diagram' (which should not be confused with diagrams showing the basic dimensions of stock). Examples of carriage diagrams, which set out the 'Circuits' for particular vehicles or sets, are also included here.

Other than trains with dining cars, which were generally made up by using special sets of coaches chosen to meet the requirements of a particular service, the composition of express trains was made up by using combinations of sets of two, three or four carriages that remained coupled together, the object being to avoid the need to make up trains from single coaches, with all the shunting that would be required. Each railway company had a maximum trainload that could be hauled, regardless of engine power, and there were specific loads for each class of locomotive over every section of line. At one time this was expressed in terms of so many axles or a certain number of vehicles, with some vehicles classed as being 'equal to 1½' or 'equal to 2'. This method of calculating train weights was rather imprecise and by the time of the Grouping had usually been replaced by a fixed tonnage for the train, with the weight of each carriage being shown on a plate, generally

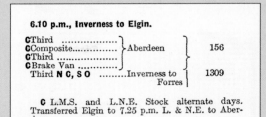

6.10 p.m., Inverness to Elgin.

C Third	⎫	
C Composite.............	⎬ Aberdeen	156
C Third		
C Brake Van	⎭	
Third N C, S O	Inverness to Forres	1309

C L.M.S. and L.N.E. Stock alternate days. Transferred Elgin to 7.25 p.m. L. & N.E. to Aberdeen.

Tonnage—115 S X, 143 S O.

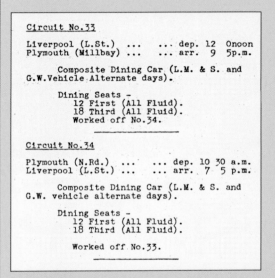

Circuit No. 33

Liverpool (L.St.) ... ... dep. 12 0noon
Plymouth (Millbay) ... ... arr. 9 5p.m.

Composite Dining Car (L.M. & S. and G.W. Vehicle alternate days).

Dining Seats –
  12 First (All Fluid).
  18 Third (All Fluid).
  Worked off No. 34.

Circuit No. 34

Plymouth (N.Rd.) ... ... dep. 10 30 a.m.
Liverpool (L.St.) ... ... arr. 7 5 p.m.

Composite Dining Car (L.M. & S. and G.W. vehicle alternate days).

Dining Seats –
  12 First (All Fluid).
  18 Third (All Fluid).

Worked off No. 33.

Left: It was not unusual for trains to be formed of different companies' stock on alternate days, in this instance the LMS and LNER. This is also taken from the June 1938 Northern Division book.

Below left: Dining Cars ran in accordance with pre-arranged 'Circuits', and this example, taken from the Breakfast Luncheon Tea and Dining Car Circuits Book dated 26 September 1938, shows how an LMS and GWR car ran between Liverpool and Plymouth on a daily basis.

Bottom left: This undated reference shows an alternative method of presenting details of dining car Circuits.

Below: This example, taken from the April 1934 LMS Western Division book, is a train made up of 'foreign' stock that does not belong to the operating company — in this case GWR vehicles.

Bottom: Another 4 July 1938 Western Division example shows the arrangements for a summer service train that started on the GWR, was transferred to the LMS and ran over joint lines for part of the journey.

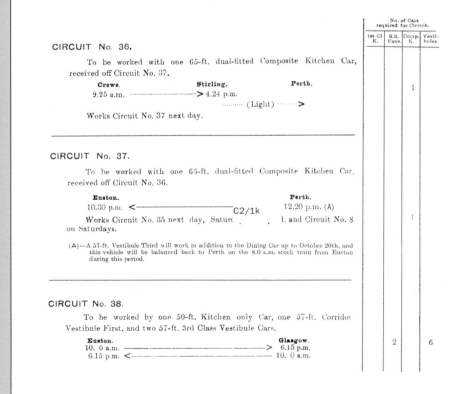

				No. of Cars required for Circuit.			
				1st Cl. K.	Kit. Vans.	Comp. K.	Vesti- bules.

CIRCUIT No. 36.

To be worked with one 65-ft. dual-fitted Composite Kitchen Car, received off Circuit No. 37.

Crewe.	Stirling.	Perth.
9.25 a.m. ————————→ 4.24 p.m.		
.... (Light) .... >		

Works Circuit No. 37 next day.

Count: 1 (Vestibules column)

CIRCUIT No. 37.

To be worked with one 65-ft. dual-fitted Composite Kitchen Car, received off Circuit No. 36.

Euston.		Perth.
10.30 p.m. ← ————— C2/1k	12.20 p.m. (A)	

Works Circuit No. 35 next day, Satur... ..., and Circuit No. 8 on Saturdays.

(A)—A 57-ft. Vestibule Third will work in addition to the Dining Car up to October 20th, and this vehicle will be balanced back to Perth on the 8.0 a.m. stock train from Euston during this period.

Count: 1 (Vestibules column)

CIRCUIT No. 38.

To be worked by one 50-ft. Kitchen only Car, one 57-ft. Corridor Vestibule First, and two 57-ft. 3rd Class Vestibule Cars.

Euston.	Glasgow.
10. 0 a.m. ————————————→ 6.15 p.m.	
6.15 p.m. ← ———————————— 10. 0 a.m.	

Count: 2 (Comp. K.), 6 (Vestibules)

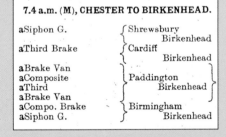

7.4 a.m. (M), CHESTER TO BIRKENHEAD.

a Siphon G.	⎧ Shrewsbury	
	⎩	Birkenhead
a Third Brake	⎧ Cardiff	
	⎩	Birkenhead
a Brake Van	⎫	
a Composite	⎬ Paddington	
a Third		Birkenhead
a Brake Van	⎭	
a Compo. Brake	⎧ Birmingham	
a Siphon G.	⎩	Birkenhead

Marshalling.		Balance.
2.40 p.m., BRISTOL TO MANCHESTER (London Road). (11.15 a.m. from Paignton.) Marshalling from Newport :—		
Two G.W. Thirds	⎧ Newport ⎩ Manchester	—
Third Brake		
Composite		
C Third Vestibule		RSD
Compo. Vestibule (12/35)	Paignton	B
Kitchen Car	Manchester	
Third Vestibule		
C Third		
Third Brake		
	⎧ Paignton	RSD
a Composite	⎨ Liverpool	D
a Third Brake	⎩ (L.St.)	

a Transferred Crewe to 6.40 p.m. to Liverpool.
B 10.20 a.m. (SO) from Liverpool.
C Until September 11th.
D 10.20 a.m. from Liverpool (SO) until September 10th; G. W. Stock unbalanced on September 18th and 25th.

Tonnage—369 Shrewsbury.
     314 Crewe.
     58 tons less on September 18th and 25th.

Express Passenger Trains

Above: The 'Irish Mail' was another famous named express passenger train that had a long history. This picture shows 'Claughton' class 4-6-0 No 5913 departing from Crewe in about 1930. Apart from the two leading vehicles, which are carrying mails and parcels, the rest of the train that can be seen is composed of passenger-carrying vehicles.
Courtesy of John Jennison

Left: To accompany the picture of the 'Irish Mail' is this close-up of part of postal vehicle No M30321, built by the Highland Railway in 1916. Some early tinplate models were made to replicate the lineside pick-up of mailbags, but I cannot recall seeing this done on a scale model. It would not be easy in a larger scale, and probably almost impossible in the smaller scales. *E. L. Vaughan*

Above left: Taken at Petts Wood in Kent, this picture shows the 'Golden Arrow' hauled by 'Merchant Navy' 4-6-2 No 35028. The 'Golden Arrow' was one of the premier express passenger trains to run in this country, although the distance covered by this Southern Region train was rather less than many of the other express train services worked in Great Britain. *P. H. Groom*

Above: This rather intriguing picture illustrates an express passenger train that consists of just three carriages, complete with nameboards, at an unknown location on the old Caledonian Railway system during the late 1920s. The train is part of an express that has been divided and No 14455, an ex-Caledonian Railway 4-4-0 that was built in 1914 and remained in service until 1954, is working this portion forward. Note the centre lamp holder carrying the 'semaphore' route indicator that was used on the Caledonian section.
Courtesy of John Jennison

Left: Despite being only a small tank engine, ex-Midland Railway 0-4-4T No 1421 is hauling a portion of a Nottingham to Derby and Llandudno express passenger train at Derby in August 1928. Although the whole train cannot be seen, it consists of probably three, perhaps four or even five carriages from Nottingham, which this engine has worked through to Derby where they will be combined with a Derby portion. The complete train will probably run via Stoke to Crewe, then over the old LNWR line to Llandudno.
Mile Post 92½ Picture Library/
A. W. V. Mace collection

Left: This 1930 view shows an Up express train departing from York with two non-passenger-carrying vehicles at the head, followed by a passenger coach, then a passenger brake-van. The rest of the visible carriages are all passenger-carrying vehicles. I can offer two possible explanations for this formation: the first is that the single carriage is a through carriage, and the second is that it is 'out of service' and being worked forward. It was not unusual to run carriages in passenger trains with the doors locked and with a suitable notice on the door windows. The locomotive is No 1665, an ex-North Eastern Railway 4-4-0 built in 1907, classified 'D20' by the LNER and withdrawn by British Railways in 1957.
Author's collection

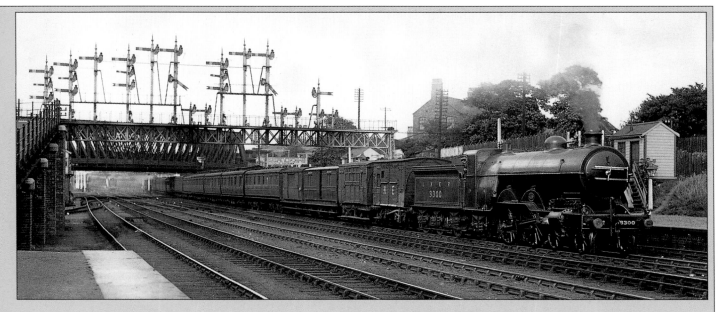

Above: This rather attractive picture of LNER No 3300 departing from York shows an ex-Great Northern Railway 4-4-2, built in 1905 and classified 'C1' by the LNER. It has been included to show a further example of an express passenger train formation that would make a fascinating model. The leading vehicles appear to be horseboxes, and the third is a passenger brake-van. The fourth is another non-passenger-carrying vehicle, which is followed by a passenger coach, which could be a 'strengthening' vehicle added to the train at York. The rest of the coaches that can be seen are plainly all clerestories, and although they cannot be made out clearly, there appears to be a passenger brake-van followed by more passenger coaches. The point is that this type of formation was not unusual on the full-size railway, but is rather rare in model form.
H. Gordon Tidey/ Lens of Sutton

Centre left: Express passenger trains are normally associated with double or multi-track lines, but this was not always the case. This picture, taken on 28 August 1939 at Whistlefield on the old North British line between Craigendoran and Ardlui, shows LNER Class K4 No 3442 at the head of an express passenger train comprising six vehicles — five are passenger vehicles, and the sixth is a passenger brake-van. *E. R. Morten*

Left: Photographed at Manchester Exchange in May 1955, British Railways Standard No 75010 is at the head of an express passenger train made up of modern stock. There is no non-passenger-carrying coaching stock at the head of this train.
B. K. B. Green

attached to the end of the vehicle. However, even after 1923 there were still some references to so many axles in certain sections of some companies' General Appendices.

While there were no doubt exceptions, in general terms it was usual to place First Class, sleeping and dining car accommodation in the centre of the train, with the dining car accommodation adjacent to the seating accommodation of the same class. However, at an earlier date some companies allowed passengers to travel throughout in the dining car; a typical example was to be found on the North Eastern Railway, which ran dining cars on express trains formed of non-corridor stock, so the dining passengers had to stay in the restaurant vehicles throughout the journey, but this was not general practice during the Grouping period. Matters became more complicated if the train was to be divided en route — it was not uncommon to have two separate dining sections that went in different directions when the train was divided.

Although we will cover this subject again in Chapter 3, there were restrictions on the use of four-wheel stock in express passenger trains; they were not permitted in trains that were timed to exceed 60mph on any part of the journey. When they were permitted there were also restrictions on where they could be marshalled in the train and the number that could be attached behind the rear brake-van over certain sections of line. As far as possible the leading vehicle of an express passenger train should be a passenger brake-van with the brake compartment leading. Other requirements included the marshalling of at least one corridor or lavatory coach when non-corridor or non-lavatory coaches were used on express trains.

Although vacuum-fitted goods stock was not permitted to run in every passenger train, it was authorised to run in some. GWR regulations taken from the 1936 General Appendix state:

'Cattle wagons having a wheelbase of 11ft 0in, 11ft 3in, or 11ft 6in, and fitted with the vacuum brake and screw couplings, may be run in passenger trains on which they are authorised to be conveyed in accordance with clause 1 of the Regulations governing the running of four-wheeled vehicles in passenger trains, except that when such cattle wagons have to be conveyed on trains which are steam heated they must be formed at the rear of the steam-heated vehicles. Any vacuum-fitted grease-box goods vehicles which may be required to work by passenger train must be specifically examined and passed by the Locomotive Department examiners and attached to trains which do not run more than 10 miles without stopping.'

What this meant was that in the steam-heating season cattle wagons without through steam-heating pipes could only run at the rear of the train, but during the non-steam-heating season they could be marshalled between the engine and the carriages, and that vans with grease axle-boxes could only be used on what were in effect branch-line or similar short-distance services.

Some restrictions applied to all classes of passenger trains: for example, care had to be taken to ensure that trains running over other companies' lines did not conflict with their requirements in respect of height or width. This also applied, of course, to the home company: each of the 'Big Four' had certain sections of line where length, height and width restrictions applied. Finally there were restrictions on the number of coaches that could be run into certain terminal stations due to reduced platform capacity. All these aspects were covered in each company's

Below: Although No 6018 is running under express passenger train headlamp code the load is only four carriages. The train is entering Kendal Castle station with the locomotive shed in the background and the goods station to the right of the picture. Note the levers in the signalbox and the two notice boards and barrow crossing; it is touches like this that make a noteworthy model. *Tony Wright*

'Ordinary, 'Residential' and Branch-line Trains

Above: 'Residential' passenger train services were usually worked by tank engines of varying sizes and wheel arrangements. This circa 1934 picture of LMS 0-6-0T No 16576 was taken when it was working an 'Ordinary' passenger train to Potters Bar — note the destination headboard. The North London Railway and later the LMS ran passenger trains from Broad Street to some LNER stations in Hertfordshire, and when the old NLR 4-4-0Ts became life-expired they were replaced by LMS Standard Class 3F tank engines, fitted with a screw reverser to make them more suitable to work stopping passenger trains.
Courtesy of John Jennison

Centre left: Branch-line locomotives were usually elderly engines that had been displaced from other more important work. There were exceptions, however: during the 1930s the GWR built some new 0-4-2Ts and 0-6-0T engines for branch-line work, but they were very similar to the locomotives they replaced. It was not until after World War 2, when the LMS introduced a series of modern tank and tender engines for this purpose, that new designs of locomotives came into service on branch-line duties. This picture, taken at Leighton Buzzard in about 1950, shows motor-fitted ex-LNWR 'Coal Tank' No 58887 with a branch train for Dunstable.
Lens of Sutton

Left: Two trains at one platform was not an uncommon phenomenon, but it is rarely seen in model form. This picture, taken at Buildwas on 15 December 1951, features two ex-Great Western locomotives, No 4406 on the 11.20am Wellington to Much Wenlock service and, nearer the camera, No 3749 on the 11.5am Craven Arms to Wellington train.
Author's collection

Above: Regardless of railway company I have always thought that the early years of the Grouping period produced some interesting train formations. This picture, taken at Perth in 1929, shows 4-6-0 'River' class No 14758 at the head of an 'Ordinary' passenger train. The leading vehicle is a horsebox and the third a passenger brake-van, while the others are passenger carriages. The three coaches at the rear appear to be a Brake Third, a Composite and an all-Third, while what seems to be an ex-Caledonian Railway coach retains its pre-Grouping colours. *Author's collection*

Left: Some coaching stock could be rather elderly, and the composition of this 'Ordinary' passenger train is not an exception to the rule. I would date this picture as circa 1925, and would suggest that all the carriages were in service by the 1880s. The locomotive, an ex-GSWR 4-4-0, entered traffic in 1900 as a renewal of an earlier class, and as LMS No 14241 it remained in service until 1929. *Author's collection*

Below left: Modern locomotives were to be seen on quite lightweight trains, and this picture of an 'Ordinary' passenger train, taken at Godley Junction on 19 May 1948, makes this point. The tare weight of the train would be about 120-130 tons, not a taxing load for No 1225, an LNER Class 'B1' built in 1947. *Author's collection*

Bottom left: Although this design of 2-6-2T originated on the LMS, No 41246 was built by British Railways, and the design, with slight modifications, was adopted as a British Railways Standard. This 1952 picture was taken at George's Road and shows the four-coach set that makes up the 5.5pm Rotherham to Manchester Central train. *Author's collection*

General Appendix to the Working Timetable or the various Sectional Appendices, which provide a wonderful source of information about how the steam railway was operated. I have often felt that one of the most useful services that could be offered by the various societies devoted to specific companies would be to make copies of their company's official documents available. I believe that both the LMS and GWR General Appendices have been reprinted commercially, and some other societies are also actively organising this, but the majority do not; in my view more could be done, and it would be of immense benefit to the hobby.

Local passenger trains, including those that ran for short distances for residential purposes, branch-line trains and passenger trains acting as feeder services for expresses, etc, were made up by using sets comprising a number of vehicles. The precise composition of the sets varied from company to company, and indeed

Below: This model of an ex-North Eastern Railway locomotive is running in pre-1928 green livery as LNER No 1870 and represents one of a pair of 'racing' engines that enjoyed the distinction of having the largest-diameter coupled wheels to be used on a steam locomotive that ran in regular service in Great Britain. This picture shows the train running in the Up direction at Marthwaite.
Tony Wright

between different parts of one company's system. For example, they might be made up of corridor, lavatory non-corridor, or non-lavatory coaches, and might be in units of two, three or more vehicles. The precise details for each would be recorded in the respective marshalling diagrams, examples of which were provided earlier in this chapter.

It is also worth pointing out that some residential rosters saw the number of coaches in a train reduced during quiet periods of the day and increased during the peak periods. The overall aim was to keep the sets working as constantly as possible. With heavy residential trains working into a busy terminus, it was not unusual for the engine that was to work a train away from the station to be accommodated in a short engine bay, and when the train arrived, either as empty coaches or as a 'turnback train', the fresh engine would move from the bay and set back on to the train. After it had departed, the engine that had brought it in would move to the bay to await the next incoming train, and so on. This arrangement usually applied to tank engines; when the arriving engine was a tender engine it would have to be turned on a turntable unless it was just working the stock to a nearby carriage siding.

It would probably be useful if I explained the principle behind the diagramming of carriage stock. The object was to run the scheduled ser-

vices using the minimum amount of stock, while bearing in mind the question of carrying capacity, quick clearance from platforms, avoiding shunting movements in stations, and where possible using the stock from an arriving train to form a departure from the same platform — avoiding as far as possible the hauling of empty coaches to take up a subsequent working, and allowing the Carriage & Wagon Department time for regular cleaning and overhaul. Adherence to the carriage diagram working was important, otherwise it could lead to additional stock having to be provided, a danger that the wrong type of stock would be used, and the cleaning margins destroyed. Replenishing gas supplies for the dining cars as well as lighting for some coaches had also to be considered. I was rather pleased to be able to publish in my book on the LT&SR a comprehensive selection of carriage diagrams for the company, which will be useful for those readers who are interested in this subject.

Although I mentioned excursion trains in the previous chapter, a further word would not be out of place. Excursion trains were run for speculative passenger traffic that was secured by advertising and local canvassing organisations, at rates that were less than the normal fare for a return journey, and covered varying periods, generally for day, half-day or evening travel. The choice of stock was largely dependent on the distance to be run and the importance of the

Top: The use of goods engines on excursion trains was commonplace. This picture was taken on 2 April 1956 and shows ex-LNER Class J39 No 64835 on the 12.20pm Leeds City to Wetherby Race Course special running with an express passenger train headcode. *Author's collection*

Above: For years the branch service from Burton-on-Trent to Tutbury was worked by a motor train, and the locomotive would have been an ex-Midland Railway 0-4-4T, but the motive power changed as the survivors were withdrawn. In this 4 June 1960 picture the locomotive, 2-6-2T No 41277, is propelling, or — according to the branding on the end of the driving trailer, 'PULL & PUSH' — pushing the train, which is the 2.35pm from Tutbury. The driver can just be seen in the centre window. *Michael Mensing*

train. Some trains required corridor stock, sometimes with dining facilities, while others comprised no more than elderly vehicles, often six-wheel carriages, that were used only a few times during the year and spent most of their time in the carriage sidings of the owning company.

If more passengers arrived than were expected, emergency arrangements had to be made, which could mean the provision at short notice of an entire train, with its crew. In these instances it would require smart work on the part of the station master and the Control Office. By the 1930s the vast majority of long-distance excursion trains were made up of corridor or vestibule coaches, sometimes with the addition of a dining car. Re-diagramming of local train circuits provided short-distance excursion trains, and these arrangements were made at the local divisional level.

More excursion trains were run during the spring and summer months than during the autumn and winter period, although we must not ignore football and other sports that generated heavy special traffic during that time of the year. Summer traffic helped the railway companies because to some extent the pressure for locomotives was less at that time of year with a reduction in freight traffic, for example coal and agricultural traffic, in particular feeding stuffs for cattle. This enabled locomotives used principally for freight traffic to be employed on some types of special or excursion trains. For example, 0-6-0 tender engines were frequently to be seen on excursion trains, in particular in the Midlands and the North of England, when large numbers of people went on holiday at the same time. This mass movement also meant that the carriages required had to be worked into the area in advance of their use and stored for anything from one to several days.

One type of passenger train that is very popular with modellers is the branch-line service, but these varied enormously. Larger centres of population could be served by regular trains that were so well patronised that it was possible to arrange something along the lines of a regular-interval service, while other services were extremely sparse. Where traffic was not heavy and a reduction in operating costs essential, one solution was to close the line to passenger traffic, but there were alternatives. As already described, during the early years of the 20th century some companies began to introduce motor trains (also known as auto-trains and reversible trains), some with the engine in the centre of the train with a driving carriage or trailer at each end, others with the engine at one end and a driving trailer at the other, for when the train was being propelled. Finally, although there were not many examples in service, we must not forget the single steam- or diesel-powered units used for this work.

One advantage of the motor train was that there was no need for the engine to run round the train; in either form it could be run into a bay platform and simply worked away in reverse. The number of carriages that could be propelled varied over the years and was subject to each company's regulations. One problem, however, was that it was often not possible to add one or more extra vehicles to cope with additional traffic needs, or an automatic-brake-fitted goods vehicle. For some reason 'pull and push' trains do not appear to have been much used in Scotland; the only example of which I am aware is the Craigendoran to Arrochar service, in the British Railways period.

Before leaving the subject of branch-line trains, we should also briefly mention mixed trains, those that carried passengers in one or perhaps two coaches but also included goods wagons. Although this class of train dates back to the early years, it remained a feature into the British Railways era. I dealt with mixed trains in some depth in the previous book in this series, so I will try not to repeat what I said there, which was taken from the LMS General Appendix, other than to say that for modellers of branch lines, this class of train has considerable potential from the standpoint of operating interest. However, the mixed train does provide an example of the principle that many aspects of train operation were similar, if not identical, for all the major British companies. The following extract is from the LNER 1947 General Appendix, and owners of the earlier book will find that the words used are similar and often identical to those of the LMS that I quoted previously:

'Mixed trains for the conveyance of goods and passengers, in which the goods wagons are not required to have continuous brake, may be run, subject to the following conditions.

'a) That the engine, tender and passenger vehicles of such Mixed trains must be provided with continuous brakes worked from the engine.

'b) That the goods wagons must be conveyed behind the passenger vehicles with brake or brake-vans in the proportion of one brake-van with a tare of 10 tons for every 10 wagons or one brake-van with a tare of 13 or more tons for every 15 wagons, or a brake-van with a tare of 16 or more tons for every 20 wagons, or fractional parts of 10, 15 or 20 wagons respectively.

'c) That the total number of vehicles of all descriptions on any such Mixed train must not exceed 30; except in the case of a Circus train when the number must not exceed 35; and

'd) That all such trains must stop at stations, so as to avoid a longer run that 10 miles without stopping; but nothing in these instructions shall require a stop to be made should the distance between them exceed 10 miles. A Circus train may, however, be run without a stop for a distance not exceeding 50 miles.'

When I compared this extract with the GWR General Appendix the words told the same story.

Although I mentioned through carriages in the previous chapter, they need to be considered within the wider context of re-marshalling passenger trains. Through carriages were vehicles scheduled to run between points that were not served by through trains. They could be carriages that remained on the parent system, or vehicles that started their journey on one com-

pany and completed it over the lines of another. Usually through carriages were scheduled services, but there were exceptions — Invalid and Picnic Saloons spring to mind, which come into the realm of special non-scheduled through workings, although I have to say that I have never seen this description used in an official document. Examples of through carriages will be found in the various extracts from the marshalling diagrams reproduced in this chapter.

Closely related to through carriages were passenger trains that were re-marshalled en route. This might be simply the addition of a horsebox, a passenger brake-van that contained luggage, or a portion of a train comprising one or more coaches. Examples of this practice will be found in this chapter, while the question of detaching horseboxes will be covered in Chapter 5, when we consider stations. If modellers wish to include re-marshalling, the track layout of the model has an important bearing on what happens, and to enable the work to be completed in the minimum amount of time a scissors crossing is probably essential.

When a passenger train arrived at a terminus — and in an operational sense a terminus did not have to be a dead-end, as some passenger services terminated at through or junction stations — there was the question of the disposal of the stock. Four options were open, and local circumstances dictated which was used:

1 The stock could be left at the station, if necessary by placing it in a siding or on another platform road.
2 It could be worked away to the carriage sidings or carriage shed. This could be done by the train engine either propelling or pulling the vehicles, depending upon circumstances, in particular the location of the sidings in relation to where the train had stopped.
3 It could be removed using a shunting engine.
4 It could be worked forward as empty stock to another station where it would become a new train.

Locomotive power in relation to train size must

not be overlooked. If the train was too heavy for a particular class of engine, a pilot or assisting engine would need to be found and coupled to the train. Before I started to write this book I always believed that the Great Western coupled the assisting engine next to the carriages and that the other members of the 'Big Four' coupled the pilot engine in front of the train engine; however, it was not quite as simple as that. The GWR General Appendix to the Rule Book of 1 August 1936 made it very clear what should happen when an assisting engine was required.

The first requirement, which would apply to all companies, was that the section of line had to be authorised for the type of engine to be used. When assisting passenger trains from the bottom to the top of an incline, the general rule was that any type of engine with coupled wheels not less than 4ft 6in might be used. On some sections it was permitted to place the assisting engine at the rear of the train provided the weather was clear, but otherwise the assisting engine would be in front of the train engine and had to be detached at the signalbox at the top of the gradient. When assistance or double-heading was required on level

Below: Another view of No 1870 running in the Down direction through Marthwaite. The train of six carriages comprises two NER clerestories, a two-coach articulated GNR set and two GCR carriages, all in LNER livery. The train represented an excursion from the North East, c1930, that had come onto the LMS at Hawes and had run via Kirby Lonsdale to join David Jenkinson's suggested branch to Kendal. *Tony Wright*

or falling gradients, 4-6-0 and 4-4-0 engines could be coupled in front of any engine (special rules applied if the train engine was a 'King' class), and where possible engines with this wheel arrangement were to be used. However, if a 4-6-0 or 4-4-0 was not available, the assisting engine — for example an 0-6-0 — was to be coupled next to the coaches. However, a 2-6-0 or 2-6-2T with 5ft 8in diameter driving wheels could be at the front of the train, unless the train engine was a 'King', and even then there were sections of line that were specified in the General Appendix where this could not be done. As someone once remarked, the GWR always had to be different from the other British railway companies!

I have personal experience of an assisting or bank engine at the rear of a train at Birmingham New Street station — where the West Pilot, usually a 4-4-0 (although earlier it would have been a 2-4-0), would bank some westbound express passenger trains away from the station to Church Road — and further west on the Lickey Incline, where all passenger trains were assisted by a banking engine. Other places that spring to mind are at Shap, Beattock and between Euston and Camden on the LMS, Cowlairs (Glasgow) on the LNER, and Parkstone, Ilfracombe, Exeter St David's to Exeter Central and Victoria to Grosvenor Bridge on the SR. I do not think there were any examples of rear-end passenger train banking on the GWR. The problem with models is that most modellers build their layouts on flat baseboards so the need for banking does not apply, but it would be rather impressive to see, and would be in keeping with my

belief that only models enable the working practices of yesteryear to be displayed in three-dimensional form.

The GWR also had different rules in respect of headlamp codes when trains were worked with an assisting engine, and from a modeller's standpoint these are worth recording. When the assisting engine was to run for distances of up to 12 miles, the engine in front was to carry one headlamp at the foot of the chimney and the train engine was to display the booked headlamps for the class of train. For distances over 12 miles the rules were that the front engine only carried the headlamps that were applicable to the class of train, and no headlamps were carried on the second engine.

Another feature, which applied to long-distance trains on all British railways, was the practice of changing engines. For example, Great Western main-line express trains from London Paddington to Birkenhead would always change engines at Wolverhampton. In my days of observing railway working, I quickly realised that the 'King' or 'Castle' class engine that worked a train from London to Wolverhampton in the morning would return to London later in the day after spending a few hours being serviced — the fire would be cleaned, the smokebox and ashpan emptied, the coal on the tender either moved forward or topped up, and the engine oiled and examined.

Another aspect of main-line passenger train working was the express train that ran into a terminus before its journey was complete. For example, the Midland Railway's Anglo-Scottish express passenger trains from St Pancras that

were required to stop at Leeds ran into Wellington station and a new engine was coupled to what had been the rear of the train; then that engine worked the train through to Carlisle, where it was changed again for the final part of the journey to the Scottish destination. This move was always noted in the Working Time Table and carriage marshalling circulars as 'reversed at Leeds'. Prior to the 1930s, when the Class 5s and 'Jubilees' were available, it was normal practice to use one engine between London and Leicester, a second engine from Leicester to Leeds, and a third from Leeds to Carlisle, but the new larger engines worked between London and Leeds, with a second engine from Leeds to Carlisle. Some other stations where trains were reversed during their journeys are given in Chapter 5 under the section that describes terminal stations.

An interesting station that has not so far been mentioned is the terminus at Bath (Green Park). Before 1930, when the locomotives of the Somerset & Dorset Joint Line were absorbed into LMS stock, there would have been the spectacle of a locomotive from one company bringing the train into the station and a locomotive belonging to another company working it forward. During this period, through trains over the S&DJR line would often contain carriages variously painted in S&D blue, LSWR green and Midland or LMS red — rather more colourful than during the British Railways era, which appears to be the favoured period for S&D modellers.

On model railways it is common practice for the locomotive to run round the carriages, and in *Railway Operation for the Modeller* I gave examples to show the correct way this should be carried out. I also gave examples of gravity shunting, where the train runs round the engine. This was the practice at Killin on the Caledonian, and Maiden Newton on the GWR. It was also used at Wellington on the LNWR & GWR Joint line, and is a feature of the model layout based on Wellington station; this is the only time that I have seen the practice reproduced in model form.

It was also not uncommon for through coaches to be attached when engines were changed; for example, Sheffield to Bournemouth carriages were attached to the 'Pines Express' at Birmingham New Street, and there were numerous other examples throughout Great Britain. There were also stations where trains ran past and reversed in, but we will deal with those in Chapter 5 when we examine different types of stations.

By modelling a real location where engine changes were carried out, the operating potential is increased, but it is also possible at fictional model locations. In broad terms, most engine changes seem to have taken place at distances of between 100 and 150 miles; for example, on the East Coast Main Line engines were often changed at Grantham, 109 miles from King's Cross, but there were exceptions, and some locomotives hauled express passenger trains over longer distances. Therefore modellers need to be mindful of what happened in

'their area', and plan accordingly. Frequently it will be found that fact is more interesting than what modellers only *believe* happened on the full-size railway.

I have never seen a model of a 'theatrical' train. They were usually run on Sundays in order to take a touring company from one theatre to another so that they arrived in good time for Monday's performance. In addition to the passenger coaches for the actors, no doubt First Class for some but Third for the majority, there would be other vehicles for the scenery and luggage that had to be taken. Open scenery trucks would need to be sheeted over in order to protect the load, while a variety of covered vehicles would convey other equipment — everything that would be necessary to enable the play to be presented at each theatre the company visited during the course of the tour. It was not uncommon for these trains to run over the rails of two companies, so engines and stock from a foreign company would be perfectly acceptable on a model.

Railway enthusiasts generally use the terms 'express trains' and 'branch trains', but a variety of other descriptions are also used. Probably the most common enthusiast term is 'semi-fast'; while not an unreasonable description, it appears to have no official basis. Another expression is 'stopper', used to describe a train that stops at all or most stations; this term originated with Steam Age trainspotters, and again has no official standing. Before considering the composition of these trains, it might be useful to consider how trains were classified and, for modellers seeking to compile a working timetable, to understand the principles behind train classification and identification.

There are three points to consider: the working timetable, the signalman's description, and the visible form of identity. The Working Time Table is the definitive document, and sets out very clearly the class of train and the times and route to be followed. However, there are many other documents that govern the working of trains, ranging from locomotive and train crew diagrams, point-to-point running times for trains that are running late, and carriage working diagrams, which were often very different from the locomotive diagrams. We will consider those that could be of interest to modellers.

For signalling purposes trains were described by telegraph using a bell code, a combination of beats on the 'block instruments' that provided the method of communication between signalboxes. Whereas it is not uncommon to see large model railways being worked by a number of operators equipped with throat mikes and in constant communication with others, the steam railway was not worked in this fashion; in the UK no use of telephones was made to describe trains, which was done only by the bell codes sent via the block instruments. However, the telephone was used to report train movements and to enable signalmen to communicate with each other, the Control Office or major marshalling yards, and for train crews to make contact with the signalbox from a point where a

telephone was provided. Many of these phones were on an open circuit and when the bell rang it was only answered by the person whose code had been used, although of course it was possible for anyone on the circuit to listen to what was being said.

The third method of describing trains was by the use of locomotive headlamps or discs. The object of using headlamps to show the classification of a train was, to quote the GWR 1936 General Appendix, to 'ensure prompt and sufficient advice being given to stations in advance in order that trains may be dealt within according to their importance'. Locomotive headlamps, which were unlit during daylight hours but were required to be lit before it became dark or in fog or falling snow conditions, were placed on the locomotive's lamp irons in various combinations, enabling railwaymen to identify the class of train. Over the years the codes changed, but examples are included here.

Discs were often used to indicate routes, and as such should not be confused with headlamp codes, although the Great Eastern section displayed the standard train classification by the use of discs. A good example of the various discs used by the LT&SR over a period of years, which may be considered as typical practice, will be found in my book on the company (see the Bibliography). The three constituents of the Southern Railway also used discs to show routes, and after 1923 the codes used by the SE&CR and LB&SCR were retained in a modified form, together with those of the LSWR, by the enlarged company. At this point I should also draw attention to the practice followed by many railway authors who, when writing captions, ignore the lamp codes carried by the locomotive and create a description based upon what they can see of the train being hauled. Usually this applies to freight trains, but passenger trains are not immune. Terms like 'van trains', 'mixed goods trains' and 'semi-fast' spring to mind. I suggest that these descriptions should be ignored and modellers should use the railway company descriptions if they wish to project an authentic picture of historical steam railways.

Earlier I used the expression 'turnback train', and readers of *Railway Operation for the Modeller* will remember that I dealt with this subject there, in particular the question of the right and wrong way to run round coaches when at a platform of a double-line station. 'Turnback train' was a general term used to describe a passenger train that arrived at a terminal and whose carriages were used to form a return service, usually with the same locomotive. It could therefore be used to describe a branchline train or one used for 'residential' services, which could also be described as an 'outer suburban passenger train', which I hasten to say is again not an official term.

Before concluding this chapter I feel that a word about headways would not be out of place. In the Introduction I mentioned the practice at model railway exhibitions of trying to ensure that something is happening all the time

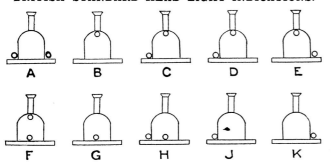

Railway Year Book.

BRITISH STANDARD HEAD LIGHT INDICATIONS.

A   B   C   D   E

F   G   H   J   K

IN 1918 the previous standard code of engine head light train classification was revised, to render the use of more than two lamps unnecessary. The present code is illustrated above. Five out of the ten former signals have not been abolished, but the other five have been changed. Previously there were four that were indicated by different positions of *three* lamps. All these have gone, and in place of them there are two signals with *two* lamps, and two with *one* lamp. In another case, namely, "G," the position of the single lamp has been altered. "C" and "D" indications are the same.

It will be seen that one lamp only is used for four different codes, "B," "G," "J," and "K." The following is the official description of each :—

A   Express Passenger train, Breakdown Van train going to clear the line, or Light Engine going to assist disabled train.

B   Ordinary Passenger train, or Breakdown Van train not going to clear the line.

C   Fish, Meat, Fruit, Horse, Cattle, or Perishable train composed of Coaching Stock. Also Goods, Mineral and Ballast trains composed entirely of Vacuum Stock.

D   Empty Coaching Stock train.

E   Fish, Meat, or Fruit train composed of Goods Stock. Express Cattle, or Express Goods train, Class A.

F   Express Cattle or Express Goods train, Class B.
    These Head Lights may also be carried by full train loads of Ballast or other materials for engineering purposes if running intact long distances.

G   Light Engine or Light Engines coupled together, or Engine and Brake.

H   Goods, Mineral, or Ballast train carrying through load to destination.

J   Through Goods, Mineral, or Ballast train stopping at intermediate stations.

K   Ordinary Goods or Mineral train stopping at intermediate stations.

As in the case of the old standard code, several railways maintain their own head light indications, especially where elaborate systems to show destinations and routes are employed, as on the London and South Western, South Eastern and Chatham, and London, Brighton and South Coast Railways. On the Great Eastern Railway special codes are used in the London area, the standard code applying elsewhere. On this line discs are used by day in lamp positions; the usual practice is, however, to use unlighted lamps by day. The Caledonian Railway uses on some sections a semaphore type of indicator by day.

44

ENGINE HEAD LAMPS.

All L.M.S. engines, whether working over the L.M.S. or other Companies' lines, and the engines of other Companies working over the L.M.S. lines, must, unless instructions are issued to the contrary, carry white head lights arranged as under, and trains must be signalled by the bell signals shown :—

Description of train.	Bell Signal.	Head Light.
1.—Express passenger train, or break-down van train going to clear the line, or light engine going to assist disabled train, or fire brigade train...	4	
2.—Ordinary passenger train, or break-down van train not going to clear the line...	3—1	
Branch passenger train (where authorised)	1—3	
Rail motor or motor train with engine leading	3—1—2	
(When running with driving compartment leading rail motors or motor trains will carry the headlamp on the same bracket as used for the tail lamp.)		
NOTE.—For arrangements in regard to electric trains see the various electric line instruction books.		
3.—Parcels, newspaper, fish, meat, fruit, milk, horse, or perishable train, composed of coaching stock	1—1—3	
4.—Empty coaching stock train	2—2—1	
Fitted freight, fish or cattle train with the continuous brake in use on NOT LESS than one-third the vehicles ...	5	
5.—Express freight or cattle train with the continuous brake on less than one-third the vehicles, but in use on four vehicles connected to the engine indicated by ✠ in the Working Time Tables	2—2—3	
Express freight or cattle train not fitted with the continuous brake, or with the continuous brake in use on LESS than four vehicles	3—2	
6.—Through freight train, or ballast train conveying workmen and running not less than 15 miles without stopping	1—4	
7.—Light engine, or light engines coupled together	2—3	
Engine with one or two brakes	1—3—1	
8.—Through mineral or empty wagon train	4—1	
9.—Freight train stopping at intermediate stations, or ballast train running short distance	3	
Branch freight train (where authorised)	1—2	
Ballast train, freight train, or officers' special requiring to stop in section or at intermediate siding in section	1—2—2	
10.—Shunting engines working exclusively in station yards and sidings.		Must, whilst in those sidings, carry one red head light and one red tail light.

The lamps must be carried in position day and night.
NOTE.—Local exceptional arrangements are shown in the respective Sectional Appendices.
When a train running on the L.M.S. Railway is worked by two engines attached in front of

---

on a layout that is on show to the public. I disagree with this approach, and believe that an interval between train movements heightens the anticipation and enjoyment of the spectacle of a well-run model railway. However, I fully accept that what I say will be rejected by some.

Part of the problem stems from the fact that because modellers can no longer observe the steam railway, certain subtleties are unknown to them. Describing programmed operations at 'Heckmondwike', when that layout was exhibited during the 1970s, will show what I mean. One sequence began when a Down stopping freight train arrived at Heckmondwike and began to shunt the yard prior to departing to the next station along the line. Before the work was completed a Down mineral train arrived and had to be shunted into the refuge siding to allow a Down express train to pass. The assumption was that the mineral train was running to time and that this move was in the working timetable. While this was happening, the stopping freight train completed its work and drew up to the yard signal ready to depart.

Once the mineral train had set back, the sig-

Locomotive headlamp codes

Above: When describing a class of train many writers look at the vehicles in the train and in effect make up a description that is based upon what they can see. In some respects I can sympathise with them — working out the precise class of train is not always easy. I think, therefore, that it is important to understand the principles behind train classification. If you are trying to build and operate an accurate model of a steam railway, it is useful to know the rules that governed the working of the full-size railway. In Chapter 1 I outlined briefly the development of passenger trains, and in my forthcoming companion title on freight train operation for the modeller we will look at goods trains, but when presenting train classification the railway companies generally put them all together into a single document. The next volume will include some further examples, but in this title I have included two. The first, taken from the *Railway Year Book* of 1922, shows the codes used at the time of the Grouping, and the second shows those in use during the 1930s up to 1950, when the final changes to the headlamp codes were made by British Railways. This example has been reproduced from the LMS 1937 General Appendix, but both the GWR and LNER were identical.

Right: In addition to the use of locomotive headlamps to show what class of train was approaching, considerable use was also made of discs, and while space does not allow examples from every company that used them, or every code that was used, I include a selection of codes in use on the Southern Railway. The source is a booklet, *Southern Railway Engine Head Codes*, dated 28 December 1943, and these examples are for the Western Section and Central Section respectively.

nal and points returned to normal and there was an interval of perhaps half a minute before the Down line signals were pulled off, then a further pause before the Down express passed. The main-line signals were then returned to danger, and the mineral train allowed to leave the siding towards the starting signal, which in due course cleared. In our imagination the signalman had allowed the mineral train to run forward, the express had run through the section in advance, and, following receipt of the 'Train out of Section' signal from the signalman in advance, the mineral had been offered and accepted and away it went. As soon as the mineral train had cleared the section in advance the stopping freight was offered, and after it was accepted the signals were pulled off again, and the train departed. This was not quite 'something happening all the time', but it was a realistic sequence of events that was in the correct order. Some may wonder why the mineral preceded the stopping freight train, but the answer is simple. If the stopping freight had gone first it would have delayed the mineral train while it was shunted into the sidings at the next station, which we assumed was about 21½ miles further along the line. By letting the mineral train go first there would be no delay to it, because it was following an express that, to use a railway term, had 'cleared the block'.

On the subject of headways, let me set out some statements from T. F. Cameron's 1946 book *An Outline of Railway Traffic Operation* and relate them to model railways. The author was Acting Divisional General Manager, Scottish Area, LNER, and he begins by pointing out that line capacity is at the very centre of efficient traffic operation. To illustrate what he means he asks his readers to imagine trains running on a circular track without any points or connections leading from it. He suggests that if the line was signalled automatically by three-aspect colour-light signals 1 mile apart, each train would require 2 miles of headway. Therefore trains running at 60mph could follow each other at 2-minute intervals and that 30 trains per hour could be run. However, the steam railway did not run trains at constant speeds, and the speed of the slowest train governed traffic movements until it could be shunted out of the way or run on to another line.

In his detailed summary, Cameron shows that in reality the railways tried to run groups of trains that travelled at the same speed, and that a slow-moving train with faster trains following would cause operational problems. On lines where there was a heavy traffic consisting of express and ordinary passenger trains and a variety of freight and mineral trains, it was necessary for the route to be equipped with independent running lines or refuge loops. The moral for modellers is that if you wish to portray an authentic model of a full-size railway, some study of prototype practice during the period you have chosen to depict and on the line upon which you are basing your model is essential. Try to imagine what is beyond the visible part of the layout and how it would affect the visible area on display.

Finally, may I end this chapter by briefly mentioning tail lamps? To a signalman the absence of a tail lamp meant that the train was not complete, and may have become divided in the section. This would not apply to a passenger train equipped with an automatic brake — if the train became divided, the brake would stop both parts — but nevertheless, until the end of steam and beyond, the presence of a tail lamp was essential. Perhaps modellers will pay more attention to this feature in future, as they are rarely seen on models of trains. What I have found is that tail lamps, when they are featured, are usually a permanent feature, and this is fine provided the lamp is at the end of the train, but it often appears at the end of a vehicle in the middle of the train, which would not be permitted on the full-size railway. The need to ensure that there was no tail lamp other than at the rear of the train was firmly impressed upon all train crews, from the moment that locomotive cleaners were passed for firing duties.

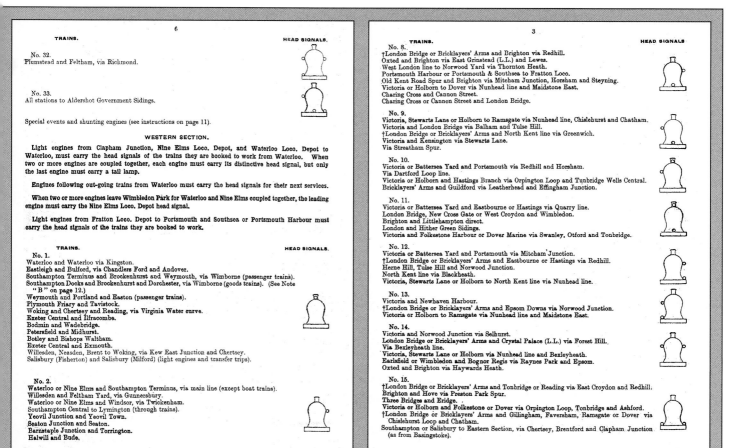

Chapter Three

Non-passenger-carrying Coaching Stock

Non-passenger-carrying coaching stock, or, as it is more commonly called, non-passenger coaching stock, comprised a group of vehicles that did not carry fare-paying passengers but were, with certain qualifications, able to run in passenger trains. (Having said that, vehicles such as prize cattle vans and horseboxes, which came within this category, usually carried grooms or stockmen to look after the animals, and I have always understood that they were not carried without a fare being paid, and that in addition they would have cattle tickets or consignment notes and waybills for the animals in their charge.)

The best description I have seen of this class of vehicle is in a section of the LNER 1947 General Appendix dealing with the conveyance of four-wheel and braked freight stock in passenger trains. This gives the requirements as:

a) oil axle-boxes
b) springs hung on brackets with links and bolts, or on hangers with auxiliary springs, or with springs bolted to the shoes
c) automatic brakes or through pipes
d) screw couplings and long buffers
e) a minimum tare weight of 6 tons

Four-wheel non-passenger-carrying coaching stock and braked freight stock conforming to the above requirements and having a wheelbase of 10ft or more (9ft until at least the late 1930s) was marked 'XP', together with the wheelbase dimension.

The terms 'piped' and 'through pipe', although more applicable to goods stock, also applied to many non-passenger-carrying coaching stock vehicles. A piped vehicle was one that was not fitted with a continuous automatic brake, and may or may not have had outside hand brakes, but which could be coupled in a train where the continuous brake pipe ran the entire length of the train and the automatic brakes could be applied by either the driver or guard.

The first vehicles in this classification dated from the earliest days of the railway, the passenger brake-van being probably the first to be constructed, although horseboxes would also date from that early period. It would perhaps be useful to begin by listing the principal types of vehicle that came into this category. The names used by different railway companies varied, and the list is not exhaustive. For example, the LMS system was slightly confusing. Many years ago David Jenkinson and I established that the LMS had two Diagram Books, one for passenger stock and the other for non-passenger-carrying stock, and our joint works on the subject were structured accordingly. For a few months prior to David's untimely death I had been researching various LMS Committee Minute Books held at the National Archive, Kew, and established that, when new construction was being authorised, some vehicles — passenger brake-vans, Post Office vans and kitchen cars — which were in the LMS Passenger Coaching Stock Diagram Book, were listed in these minutes as Non-passenger-carrying Coaching Stock. Therefore, to avoid confusion, I will adhere to the classifications that we have published.

Non-passenger-carrying Coaching Stock

Aeroplane Van
Bogie Parcels Van
Bullion Van
Corpse Van
Covered Combination Truck
Covered Milk Van
Fish Van and Open Trucks
Fruit and Milk Van
Horse Box
Insulated Milk Van
Insulated Sausage Van
Kitchen Car
Luggage and Parcels Van
Milk Van
Milk Tank (including various underframes for conveying road tanks)
Bogie container flats for the Euston, Fleetwood to Belfast service
Motor Car Van
Open Carriage Truck
Passenger Brake Vans
Post Office Carriages (TPO), Sorting and Stowage Vans
Prize (or Special) Cattle Van
Theatrical Scenery Truck (both covered and open)
Ventilated Insulated Meat Van

In theory any of these vehicles could run in an ordinary passenger train and, subject to certain restrictions, in an express passenger train. In reality this did not happen, and the regulations that applied in 1937 may be considered as being fairly typical for the post-1923 era. Trains made up of non-passenger-carrying coaching stock were not allowed to exceed 25 vehicles in the

Above: Photographed on 12 August 1967 at Delaney Sidings near Skipton, Class 5 No 45273 is at the head of a Class C train composed entirely of vehicles conforming to coaching stock requirements. The composition of this train is typical for the period, a mixture of passenger brake-vans and general utility or similar bogie vans, with the rich variety of the earlier years absent. *Paul Cotterell*

Centre right: This lengthy train of non-passenger coaching stock comprises a mixture of four- and six-wheel vehicles — there does not appear to be any bogie stock — and was photographed near Bedford in 1923. It would have been possible to see a very similar train 10 or even 20 years later — the lifespan of these vehicles was generally about 40 years, although by then bogie vehicles would probably form part of the train. Passenger brake-vans, open and covered combination trucks, fruit and milk and parcels vans can all be identified in this train. *Author's collection*

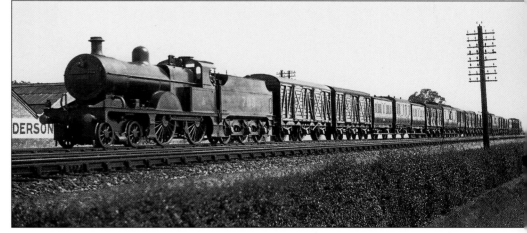

Right: Certain rules applied to where four-wheel vehicles could be marshalled in a train. This horsebox has an 11ft wheelbase — note the branding below the letters 'XP' on the right-hand door — and it has been marshalled at the head of the train. *G. Hunter*

Left: It is perfectly possible to include in the same train both non-passenger-carrying coaching stock and goods stock, provided they have suitable buffers, couplings, springing and brakes, or through pipes. Of the vehicles that can be identified here, four are non-passenger coaching stock vehicles and eight are goods stock. *Courtesy of John Jennison*

Top: This long train, hauled by Midland Railway Class 2 4-4-0 No 346, was taken in the mid-1920s and shows an empty stock train. The picture was taken at LNW Junction, Derby, and the train is probably the 3.50pm Derby to Gloucester. There are a number of passenger brake-vans, at least one fruit and milk van, and there also appears to be one six-wheel passenger carriage. Not all the vehicles are LMS, and at this date it would not be unreasonable to find that both pre- and post-Grouping liveries would be carried by the stock in this lengthy train. *Courtesy of John Jennison*

Above: Photographed at South Kenton in the late 1930s is a train running under the headlamp code that was described in the LMS General Appendix as 'Parcels, newspaper, fish, meat, fruit, horse or perishable train composed of coaching stock'. This description certainly applies to the three carriages at the rear — two certainly — and I think the centre one is also a passenger brake-van. At first sight the two leading vehicles may be mistaken for low goods wagons, but in fact they are open carriage trucks, one loaded with a lift van, the other a container that has been securely roped to the truck. The main reason for including this picture is to show a train of this class running as a special with a reporting number, 537, on a board on the top lamp holder. The fact that the lift van belongs to a furniture removal firm suggests that this may possibly be a large household removal. The locomotive is ex-LNWR 'Prince of Wales' 4-6-0 No 25791. *Author's collection*

case of milk, parcels and horseboxes with passenger carriages; if the train was comprised entirely of horseboxes, milk tanks or fish vans, 30 was the maximum. Unlike goods trains, when the length was quoted without a brake-van, the numbers given above included any brake-vans that might be part of the train.

Four-wheel vehicles were subject to certain restrictions when they were part of an express train. Indeed, there were some express trains from which they were totally excluded, but if they were permitted the wheelbase had to be at least 10ft (9ft until the late 1930s). When four-wheel vehicles were permitted they had to be marshalled at the rear of all bogie vehicles provided for the conveyance of passengers, but where this was not practicable they could be

Above: This ordinary passenger train headed by an ex-LNWR 'Jumbo', running as LMS No 5012 *John Ramsbottom,* is a mixture of passenger and non-passenger-carrying vehicles. This locomotive was often rostered to work the 1.10pm from Barrow on Furness, although in this instance it is not on that particular working. *Tony Wright*

marshalled next to the engine. The intermixing of four- and six-wheel vehicles next to the engine was permitted provided that they were marshalled in front of the bogie vehicles. On special trains conveying theatrical parties, or Army, Navy or Air Force specials, the restrictions were relaxed and four-wheel vehicles could be marshalled in the train according to destination.

Vehicles that had a wheelbase of 15ft or more, fitted with oil axle-boxes, automatic brakes or a through pipe, screw couplings and long buffers, and with a minimum tare weight of 6 tons, could be marshalled anywhere in the train, but open fish and open carriage trucks that were less than 21ft in length over the headstocks were prohibited from working in express passenger trains. There was a total restriction on the inclusion of bogie freight vehicles or empty one-plank freight wagons fitted with automatic brakes in any passenger train.

The 1930s saw the introduction of milk tank wagons, at first running on four wheels but later converted to run on six wheels. The latter were not subject to any restrictions and could be worked on any passenger train other than those where special restrictions applied. Four-wheel tanks could not be included in any train that was

scheduled to exceed 60mph at any point of the journey, and when they were permitted they had to have a six- or eight-wheeled vehicle immediately behind them.

Non-passenger-carrying coaching stock was often included in passenger trains, and I have included a number of pictures to illustrate various formations. It was also possible to see a complete train made up of one class or type of vehicle, plus a brake vehicle. Examples include milk trains made up of tank wagons with perhaps some milk vans to cater for churn traffic, and complete trains of fish vans. Fruit was another traffic that sometimes required special trains, a subject that I explored in some detail in my book on the Ashchurch to Barnt Green line (see the Bibliography). Readers interested in learning more about fruit traffic from the Evesham area, which was sent to many destinations across Great Britain, will find a summary of my findings in that book, but it should be pointed out that while such non-passenger stock was usually described as 'Fruit & Milk' there were also automatically braked or through-pipe fruit vans that were classified as goods stock, and both types could be used in special fruit trains.

In the days before racehorses travelled by road to the racecourse they went by rail, and a complete special train of horseboxes, with perhaps one passenger carriage, might be provided. Parcels traffic would require complete parcels trains, and examples of the composition of the trains and the re-marshalling that took place were given in Chapter 2. These trains could include CCTs, luggage and parcels vans, but they were largely made up of passenger brake-vans. Postal trains, often described as TPOs

(Travelling Post Offices), were run on behalf of Royal Mail, but because they ran at night, pictures of these trains are rather rare. Another special traffic that could require special trains was for homing pigeons. This traffic could range from a basket of birds sent under the guard's care in a passenger brake-van to several vehicles running as a special train to the place where the birds were to be released. Another class of rather infrequent special train was the Circus train, which was used by both Bertram Mills and Billy Smart. The formation comprised horseboxes, special cattle vans, motor car vans, CCTs, elephant vans and passenger coaches.

Non-passenger-carrying coaching stock has always fascinated me and I believe that trains made up from this class of stock are both interesting to see and offer very considerable operating potential for most modellers. The act of attaching or detaching vehicles at stations helps to fulfil the concept that you must keep things moving, but those modellers who use automatic couplings should remember that the act of uncoupling the vacuum or Westinghouse pipes, then the screw couplings, took time, and during the steam heating season there might also be the heating pipes to uncouple. The sequence would be first the automatic brake pipe, then the heating pipes and finally the screw couplings, so please pause to allow the viewer to appreciate that you are representing this work taking place. Finally, do not forget that when the engine has backed up to the train the vacuum for the automatic brake has to be restored; this also takes time, so the sight of an engine backing up to a train and immediately setting off destroys the illusion of reality in miniature.

Top: This picture illustrates the difficulty of trying to put everything into neat and tidy categories. At first sight this is a parcels train, but the locomotive headlamp code of one lamp at the top of the smokebox door confirms that it is an 'Ordinary' passenger train. The date is about 1925 and this train, the 2.38pm from Manchester Central to Derby, is at Breadsall Crossing. The formation is rather interesting: two six-wheel covered combination trucks, a passenger brake-van, three more covered combination trucks, a Midland Railway four-coach set comprising Third Brakes at each end with a Composite and an all-Third between, and finally what appears to be a horsebox at the rear of the train. *Author's collection*

Above: This LMS-period picture shows an Up express between Ratcliffe Junction and Kegworth, and illustrates the practice of including non-passenger-carrying stock in passenger trains. The two leading vehicles are vans: the first appears to have end doors so is maybe carrying a motor car, while the second is probably a fruit and milk van. The third is an open carriage truck with a sheeted load, a not unusual practice but not one that I have ever seen reproduced in model form, followed by a covered combination truck. The next three are passenger-carrying vehicles, the fourth a passenger brake-van, and finally six passenger-carrying coaches to complete the train. *W. L. Good*

Above: The movement of milk was an everyday affair and all the major British railway companies worked milk trains. Prior to the introduction of milk tank wagons, at first running on four wheels, but later on six, milk was carried in churns, and although this gave flexibility for small consignments, it was not the most economical way to convey this traffic. For modellers of branch lines, 'churn traffic' can be part of the scene, but for those with main-line 1930s or later models, complete milk trains can be featured. Here ex-LNWR 4-6-0 No 25678 heads a train of two six-wheel and three four-wheel milk tanks at Ashton in 1934. These are followed by a passenger brake-van, no doubt loaded with milk churns and also carrying the guard. The final three vehicles are two six-wheel covered milk vans and another passenger brake-van, all probably loaded with churn traffic. *L. Hanson*

Centre right: Another ex-LNWR 'Prince of Wales' 4-6-0, No 25641, is seen in this mid-1930s picture taken at Tebay. I believe the three leading LMS vans and those at the rear are loaded with churn traffic, with the milk tanks in the middle of the train. The passenger brake-van is at the rear of the train, which is a little unusual; generally the guard had a better and steadier 'ride' if his brake-van was 'inside' the train, with other vehicles behind. Finally, it is worth pointing out that although these two pictures show ex-LNWR 4-6-0s, a few years later the train engine would probably have been a Stanier Class 5. *Author's collection*

Right: The third milk train picture was taken in 1944 at Elstree and shows LMS Compound No 1164 with a train of milk tank wagons and some passenger brake-vans at the rear for the churn traffic. I am not sure whether the number 643, chalked on the smokebox door, is a special train number for this train, or has simply not been removed from a previous working. *Author's collection*

Above Left: This is the type of train that should appeal to many modellers — a horsebox special. No 304 is on the Up line of the Lickey Incline approaching Blackwell and is being assisted in the rear by a bank pilot engine. The train is interesting: the carriage at the rear is a passenger vehicle with a brake compartment and appears to be an old GWR coach. If so, this special train of six horseboxes could have originated on the GWR system and been handed over to the Midland Railway at either Gloucester, Cheltenham or Worcester to be worked forward by a Midland locomotive and men. Although I have used a Midland era picture, it represents the practice that was followed by all the British companies, and it is worth noting that horsebox specials could run over the lines of more than one railway company, or be confined to just one.

Centre left: Although the majority of pictures used in this chapter are post-1923 views from the LMS group of companies, here are two of what today we would call 'East Coast' trains. The first was probably taken just prior to 1923 and the other is an LNER-period picture, but both show that the general composition of parcels trains was similar to those of the LMS; in my opinion it was the date rather than the owning company that governed the composition of this class of train. Another feature of the first picture is that it confirms the longevity of many British railway locomotives: No 1321 was built by the Great Northern Railway in 1898 and became LNER No 4321 after the 1923 Grouping. In 1946 the LNER renumbered it and it ran as No 2152 until British Railways withdrew it from service in 1949. The lesson to be learned is that many model railways are operated by stock that is too modern and whose average age is too low.

Left: This early Grouping era picture shows a North Eastern Railway 4-4-2 running as LNER No 722 at the head of a parcels train. The first three vehicles are goods stock, fitted with either through brake pipes or automatic brakes, followed by five coaching-stock vehicles that all appear to be passenger brake-vans. *Author's collection*

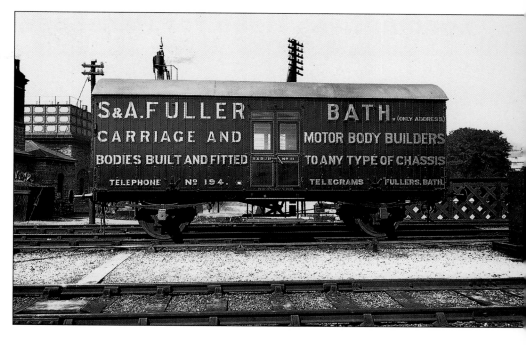

Above: From the earliest years privately owned wagons, usually for coal traffic, were a regular sight on British railways and as such they will be included in *Freight Train Operation for the Railway Modeller*. However, I felt that this colourful example of what appears to be a privately owned van, equipped to run in passenger trains, should be included in this chapter. Although few in number, there were some vehicles, generally motor car vans or covered combination trucks, that carried advertising; a latter-day example of this class of vehicle would be the various Palethorpe's sausage vans built by the GWR and LMS during the late 1930s. This example was based upon an existing Midland Railway design of covered combination truck, but in order that it could run anywhere in Great Britain it was dual-fitted — equipped with both Westinghouse and vacuum brakes. This Somerset & Dorset Joint Railway vehicle was photographed in August 1909 and was probably painted in the blue body colour used by that company for its coaching stock. *NRM Derby Collection, DY 9125*

Above:
Egg traffic went by passenger train or express freight train. This label was produced for the Midland Railway.

Left:
Homing pigeon traffic could vary from a single basket of birds to a complete train. The railway companies used special labels, like this LMS example.

Chapter Four

Locomotives Used for Passenger Trains

If you ask modellers with working layouts what their most important asset is, I would expect the answer to be their locomotives. In this respect their views are similar to those of the full-size railways where, other than the actual railway — what today is described as the 'infrastructure' — the locomotives were their most important asset. Without locomotives the trains could not run, and if the trains did not run, revenue could not be generated. The difference between the full-size railway and many models is that on the latter we can sometimes see what might be called 'interesting prototypes'. Perhaps I should expand upon what I mean.

The constraints on the full-size railway were many — the introduction of particular classes of locomotives to work over a certain section of line was often outside the control of the CME or Locomotive Superintendent, while some bridges or other structures did not permit the most modern classes to run — but generally these do not apply to model railways. I have always felt that the most realistic approach is to stay as close to prototype practice as possible, even if it means that your model will not see a particular class in action. However, there is a way round this rather constricting approach, and two of my friends called it 'the funny trains'.

My first introduction to this concept came many years ago when the late Gavin Wilson demonstrated his Highland Railway layout to me; then, after working through the sequence, he brought out of the hidden sidings models of trains that, by and large, would not be seen on that line. I no longer remember their precise composition, except for his model of the Royal Train, which made a splendid sight. This 4mm-scale model of the complete train is now part of the model collection at the NRM. The late David Jenkinson, also a close friend of Gavin Wilson, developed the idea of 'funny trains' on his

Kendal Castle layout, and the parade was worth watching. In my view, provided a modeller generally tries to present an authentic approach and separates fact from fiction, this is a reasonable approach to take. While I have never wanted to construct 'out-of-period' trains, I freely admit that there are a number of locomotives I would like to own that would never have been seen side by side in reality.

To return to the theme of this chapter, the object is briefly to review passenger train working during the steam era, generally using pictures to illustrate the theme. However, limitations of space mean that it would be impossible to illustrate all the wheel arrangements described in the text or all classes that ran in passenger service. Readers will note that my choice tends to err towards what I consider to be 'interesting' within the context of this work, rather than to feature just the most popular modern classes.

We will begin by taking a brief look at the changing face of the locomotive stock of the various British railways during that period. In Chapter 1 I explained, with particular reference to the carriage stock development, why I felt that 1899 was a pivotal point in the history of the British steam railway. In this chapter I want to examine many of the various types of locomotives that were used to haul passenger trains during both the 19th and 20th centuries, and, as we will see, two wheel arrangements, the 4-4-0 during the 19th century and the 4-6-0 from the early 1900s, were preferred by the majority of railway companies for important passenger trains. Of course there were exceptions, but in terms of sheer numbers they can be considered as the two classic wheel arrangements for this type of work.

During the early years of the steam railway, locomotives were considered to be either 'passenger' or 'goods' engines. The first use I have

found of the term 'mixed traffic' is dated 1879, and was used in the specification for the LT&SR 4-4-2T engines, which were also described as 'Universal' engines. If we try to use the Whyte notation to classify the very first locomotives, it is not easy. Suffice to say that they mostly ran on four wheels and could be described a 0-2-2 or 2-2-0 tender engines. Readers interested in this era of railway history are recommended to read E. L. Ahrons's classic work listed in the Bibliography, which will provide them with an excellent review of the development of steam locomotives during the early years.

The first example of what became the initial type of standard express passenger engine, the 2-2-2, appeared in 1833, and locomotives with this wheel arrangement continued to be built until 1894. The final example was constructed by the Great Northern Railway, and although the GWR was building double-frame 2-2-2s during 1891–2, they were soon altered to become 4-2-2s. The increasing weight of trains, described earlier, meant that the 2-2-2-wheel arrangement was soon outdated and by the end of 1914 none of this type remained in service.

During the early years a number of locomotives were built with unusual wheel arrangements, but they had little or no effect on the mainstream of development and need not be considered in this review. Therefore the next wheel arrangement we must examine is the 2-4-0. In 1848 the classic British inside-cylinder engine with the trailing axle behind the firebox was introduced, and later examples of this wheel arrangement survived into the early days of British Railways. At first they were used on goods traffic, but soon 2-4-0s were to be found on many of the best passenger trains. The next logical development came in 1860 when the first 4-4-0s were built — in the pre-Whyte notation era they were known as 'Passenger

Top to Bottom:

The classic arrangement of an inside-cylinder engine with the trailing axle behind the firebox was introduced in 1848 and examples of the 2-4-0 wheel arrangement were to remain in service for more than 100 years. To illustrate this type I have chosen a picture of an old Great Eastern Railway Class E4 locomotive, built in 1902 and not withdrawn until 1958. No 62797 is seen at Aylsham on 7 June 1952 on the 2.10pm Dereham to Norwich Thorpe train. *Author's collection*

A variation of the 2-4-0 was the 0-4-2, and although the absence of a leading bogie or pony truck may appear to have been a disadvantage on express passenger trains, this did not prove to be the case. Here we see a pre-1923 picture of a London, Brighton & South Coast Railway 'Gladstone' 0-4-2, one of a class built between 1882 and 1891. *Author's collection*

The first use of the 4-4-0 wheel arrangement was in 1860, and 'passenger engines with leading bogies', as they were originally known, were still in service a century later. To illustrate this type I have chosen GWR 'City' class No 3441, photographed near Hayes (Middlesex) when working an express passenger train. The use of double frames on passenger engines was not common, which is another reason for including this picture. *Author's collection*

There are two reasons for including this picture. The first is to show a tender weatherboard on a passenger engine; they were usually found on freight engines, but could also be fitted if the engine was used to run tender-first on passenger trains. The second reason is to show the articulated carriages. The locomotive is an ex-Great Central 4-4-0, now LNER Class D7 No 5710, seen at Sheffield Victoria in May 1929. Built in 1892, this engine was withdrawn in 1930. *W. L. Good*

Left: The single-driving-wheel engine may look very old-fashioned, but 2-2-2s were to remain in service for 81 years, which is rather longer than the more glamorous Pacifics! This is ex-Midland Railway locomotive No 39, built in 1864 and withdrawn from service in 1893. *Author's collection*

Right: David was always interested in the 10 locomotives of the Midland Railway '990' class 4-4-0s and I recall that when we met he already owned an EM model of one of the class. This shows No 809 as renumbered by the LMS on a Down Ordinary passenger train from Dents Head to Kendal Castle. *Tony Wright*

Engines with Leading Bogies'. Locomotives of this wheel arrangement were to be constructed well into the Grouping era by three of the 'Big Four' companies, and the final survivors ran until the early 1960s.

Although the 2-4-0 and 4-4-0 wheel arrangements had been successfully introduced, some railways continued to construct 2-2-2s, and there was a strong belief that the 'single-wheel' engine was more suited to work the fastest passenger trains. The logical development of the 2-2-2 was the 'bogie single', or 4-2-2, and the first examples to enter service appeared on the Great Northern Railway from 1870. Probably the most famous of the 'bogie singles' were those built by the Midland Railway between 1887 and 1900 to the designs of S. W. Johnson, although I have no doubt that supporters of the GWR and GNR may have different views! The continued construction of what could be considered by then as an outdated design was due to the introduction of steam sanding, which helped to prevent the large driving wheels from slipping. However, as with the earlier single-wheel engines, the increasing weight of trains proved to be too much for them and during the Edwardian period they began to be relegated to pilot duties and less onerous work.

The final decade of the 19th century saw the LNWR introduce 'Compound' 2-2-2-2s and the LSWR 4-2-2-0s, but again they had no real effect on the mainstream of express passenger locomotive development, and it was the 4-4-2, introduced by the GNR in 1898, that marked the way forward. Although this design was followed by the L&YR's 4-4-2s in 1899, these were inside-cylinder engines and as such a dead end — the future for express passenger engines lay with two outside cylinders, or three or four cylinders outside and between the frames. Although I consider the 4-6-0 to be a 20th-century design, it should be noted that the first use of this wheel arrangement was on the Highland Railway in 1894 for goods traffic, and 1900 on the North Eastern Railway for express passenger work.

In many respects the 19th century is not difficult to summarise as far as express passenger tender locomotives are concerned; however, tank engine wheel arrangements are more difficult. As Ahrons so neatly put it, 'There has always been more scope for variations of tank engine design, especially in the wheel arrangements, than in the case of tender engines.' The story is so complex that I have not tried to mention every wheel arrangement used by every company, but rather to provide a flavour of the modelling potential that is open to those who are not confined to the era of British Railways.

Above: The logical development of the 'single' was the 'bogie single', and I have resisted the temptation to use a picture of a Midland engine to represent this type, even though they were probably the most famous example of this wheel arrangement to run in this country. When the increasing weight of passenger trains made it impossible for 'bogie singles' to work principal express services, some were used on lighter duties, as seen here. The line between Liverpool and Manchester was ideal for a 'single' pulling a moderate train, and No 970, a Great Central engine built in 1900 and withdrawn in 1924, is seen near Padgate with an express passenger train. *Author's collection*

Left: The ex-Furness Railway 4-4-0 now running as LMS No 10333 is at the head of an Ordinary passenger train made up of some rather elderly carriages. As stated elsewhere in this book, carriages had long lives and this train, with the engine in Crimson Lake livery, is very typical of secondary services in the 1920s. *Tony Wright*

Below left: This magnificent model of a Midland Railway '2183' class 4-4-0 was built by the late Ken Woodhead and represents a class that both David and I greatly admired. The locomotive is standing outside the locomotive shed at Kendal Castle, which was based upon the brick-built shed at St Albans. *Tony Wright*

Tank engines used for passenger work ran with either four, six or eight wheels coupled. The latter were really freight engines, but they were also used for some passenger work; two examples were the GNR 0-8-2Ts, which did not last long on this work, and the LNWR 0-8-4Ts, sometimes used on passenger trains in South Wales during the post-1923 period. Other classes of freight tank engines used for passenger work that spring to mind are the GWR's 0-6-2Ts and the LNWR's 'Coal Tanks'. From about 1860 a number of different tank engine designs were introduced and, given the longevity of many designs from the 1860s and in particular the 1870s-1880s, these Victorian-era locomotives would be at home on many post-1923 layouts. For this reason I am not going to separate passenger tank engines into pre- or post-1899, but rather to review the developments that took place over the years.

Of the six-wheel engines with a rigid wheelbase, the 2-4-0T type was popular with a number of companies and was at first preferred to the 0-4-2T arrangement, which survived on the old GWR system until almost the end of steam. As an alternative to side tanks, some varieties were built with well or saddle tanks, and later the pannier tank arrangement was used by the GWR. The logical development of the 2-4-0T and 0-4-2T was the 2-4-2 tank engine. The first examples of this wheel arrangement entered service in 1863, and probably its most successful use was on the L&YR, where locomotives of this type were in service until well into the British Railways era.

Although the 4-4-0T wheel arrangement was not built in large numbers, it was to be found on the North London, Caledonian, Highland, North British, Metropolitan and District Railways. Even the LSWR, SER, LNWR and Midland Railway owned a few, and an example of one of them would be on my personal 'funny trains' list. The reverse arrangement, the 0-4-4T, first appeared on the South Eastern Railway, and while the 4-4-0T was not built in large numbers, the 0-4-4T was. The final example to appear was built by the LMS in January 1933, some years after other companies had ceased to construct engines of this type; however, examples were still in British Railways

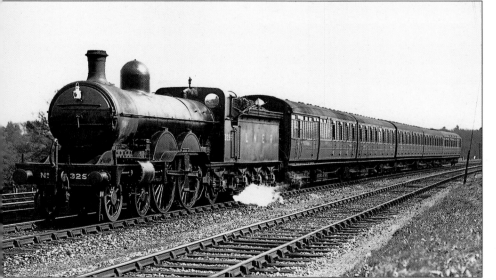

Above: The natural enlargement of a 4-4-0 was by either adding another pair of driving wheels to produce a 4-6-0 or a pair of carrying wheels, as illustrated here. This picture of an ex-Great Northern Railway locomotive, now LNER Class C2 No 3255, represents the 4-4-2 or Atlantic wheel arrangement that was used by a number of British railway companies. This undated, but probably mid-1920s, picture shows it working an 'Ordinary' passenger train. *Author's collection*

Left: The 2-4-0T wheel arrangement was used by a number of British railway companies, and I could not resist including this delightful picture of Millwall Extension Railway No 6 at Millwall Junction on the Great Eastern Railway. It is fitted with a Westinghouse brake and was perfectly capable of working light passenger trains over the branch to the terminus at North Greenwich. *K. Nunn*

Below left: The 2-4-2T wheel arrangement was a development of the 2-4-0, and the engines of that wheel arrangement built by the Lancashire & Yorkshire were among the most successful. This picture of No 10640 near Fleetwood shows an engine that has been motor-fitted. *Author's collection*

Bottom left: The Metropolitan & Great Central Joint station at Quainton Road is the setting for this late-1920s picture of an LNER Class F7, an ex-Great Eastern Railway 2-4-2T that was built in 1909 and remained in service until 1948. In 1924 it was motor-fitted and transferred to the Great Central section. Transfers of locomotives between the constituent companies of the 'Big Four' were not uncommon after the Grouping. *Gordon Stuart*

Top right: The GWR's 2-4-2T engines were not one of that company's most successful designs. However, I have included this picture of No 3629 at Hooton, on the LMS & GWR Joint line between Chester and Birkenhead, in order to show a very different design of this wheel arrangement. *Author's collection*

Top far right: There was something delightfully archaic about the old North London Railway's locomotives and passenger carriages. The 4-4-0T was not widely used, but probably more locomotives of this wheel arrangement ran on the NLR than on any other British railway. The picture was taken during the early 1900s and the train would be running from Broad Street to Richmond. *Author's collection*

Centre right: Unlike the 4-4-0T, the 0-4-4T was built in large numbers and the final examples did not appear until 1933. The Midland Railway used this type across the system and many of the class came into British Railways ownership. No 58046 was originally No 1298, and when this picture was taken on 20 August 1949 it was motor-fitted and working a Burnham to Templecombe passenger train. Note the headlamp code: on some lines, and the S&D was one, a simplified headlamp code was used.
Author's collection

Right: This delightful picture of an ex-Caledonian Railway 0-4-4T illustrates the type of pre-Grouping engine that was used on some branch-line passenger services into the British Railways era, although in the case of No 15103 it was withdrawn in 1945.
Author's collection

service during the 1950s, including some dating from the previous century.

Although the six-wheels-coupled tank engine is normally associated with goods and shunting work, engines with this wheel arrangement were also used to work passenger trains. The LMS and in particular the GWR employed their standard designs on passenger trains, but probably the most famous of all 0-6-0 passenger tank engines were the Stroudley 'Terriers', built to work on the South London line; when displaced due to the increasing weight of trains, they found employment on branch trains on the Southern Railway. The logical development of the 0-6-0 was to add a trailing radial axle-box, and the first locomotives of this type built for passenger train work appeared on the L&YR in 1879, closely followed by the LNWR, where many locomotives with this wheel arrangement were built for both goods and passenger work, with examples remaining in service until after Nationalisation.

The first main-line express passenger tank engines were the highly successful 4-4-2Ts built for the LT&SR in 1880, a design that was enlarged and improved over the years and as such remained in service on the 'Tilbury' section until the British Railways era. These were to pave the way for other wheel arrangements of express passenger tank engines. Although the 0-4-4 and 2-4-2 types continued to be built, after 1900 the developments were largely in the realms of six-coupled engines to cope with the heavier trains, and during the years that followed, two wheel arrangements were highly successful: the 2-6-2T and 2-6-4T. The first 2-6-2Ts were built by the GWR, and developments of the original design were still entering service after 1948, while the highly successful 2-6-4Ts, as designed by the LMS, although it was not the first railway company to use this wheel arrangement, were to be further developed and constructed into the 1950s by British Railways.

The period from 1900 to the Grouping of 1923 also saw the construction of passenger tank engines with a variety of wheel arrangements. None was constructed in large numbers

Above: This is probably my favourite picture of David's layout. Although when this picture was taken, the full complement of station seats, platform barrows and trolleys and other items normally found at stations of this size were not in place, the potential can be seen. The cast pillars and roof, which was made by using Plastikard strip and glazing material, was a work of great skill. For the record, the locomotive is No 15051, the ex-Highland Railway 0-4-4T also seen on page 33. *Tony Wright*

Left: In some respects the obvious choice for an 0-6-0T on a passenger train would be a GWR pannier tank engine, but I felt that an alternative could be another class of GWR 0-6-0 tank, one from a railway that became part of the GWR in 1923. This picture was taken in about 1922 and shows Brecon & Merthyr Railway No 18 leaving Merthyr with the 2.50pm train to Newport. This saddle tank was built in 1881 and shortly after this picture was taken it became GWR No 2191. *K. Nunn*

Below left: One of the most successful classes of passenger tank engines to be built was the LB&SCR Class I2. This picture was taken at Woking in 1930 and shows Southern Railway No 15 with a passenger train. *J. A. G. H. Coltas*

and few could be really considered to be highly successful, but as models some would be rather impressive. These large tank engines included the following:

0-6-2T	GNR and GER
0-6-4T	Midland, SE&CR, Metropolitan and NSR
2-6-2T	L&YR (an unsuccessful design of inside-cylinder engine)
2-6-4T	SE&CR
4-4-2T	GCR, GNR, GWR, LNWR, Furness, LB&SCR and NBR
4-4-4T	Metropolitan and NER (the latter also being converted to 4-6-2T form)
4-6-0T	NER (some later converted to 4-6-2T form)
4-6-2T	LB&SCR, LNWR, Caledonian and GCR
4-6-4T	LT&SR, GSWR, Furness, LB&SCR and LMS (L&YR design)

Above left: During the early 1900s and until the Grouping a number of different wheel arrangements for passenger tank engines were built, but none could be considered to have been very successful. To represent this varied group of locomotives I have selected the ex-Furness Railway 4-6-4T, a class that entered traffic in 1920 and was withdrawn between 1934 and 1940. This picture of No 11101, running with an express passenger train headcode, was taken at Carnforth circa 1925. *H. Gordon Tidey*

Left: The most successful passenger tank engines to be built were probably the 2-6-2 and 2-6-4 wheel arrangements. To show both types I have selected three pictures, the 2-6-2T being represented by LNER 'V1' No 7658 at Consett on 2 August 1948 when it was working the 4.5pm 'Ordinary' passenger train to Newcastle. *W. A. Camwell*

Below: This undated but pre-World War 2 picture of LMS Class 4P No 2449 with an 'Ordinary' passenger train is an example of the series of 2-6-4T engines built by the LMS from 1927 onwards. They were excellent machines and formed the basis of the later British Railways Standard design. *Author's collection*

Apart from the continued construction of some pre-1923 designs, the Grouping era can be considered as being largely either a time of 2-6-2 or 2-6-4 tank engines for main-line work, with smaller 0-6-0Ts and 0-4-2Ts built by the GWR for branch-line work. However, we must not forget that the LMS introduced a modern 2-6-2 tank engine in 1946, and these engines, intended to replace old and worn-out examples for branch-line work, were the basis of a British Railways design. In many respects the post-1923 passenger tank engines lack the variety of the earlier years, but that applies to many other aspects of our railway history during the Grouping period.

Earlier I mentioned that the 4-6-0 was the classic wheel arrangement for important passenger train work during the 20th century, and I ought to clarify this statement. According to O. S. Nock in his *British Locomotives of the 20th Century* (see the Bibliography), at the end of the 19th century there were only 22 locomotives of this type in service, or 27 if you regard 31 December 1900 as the end of the century, as I do: 2 GWR, 10 NER and 15 HR. By the end of 1919 the number had risen to 976. Of this total, more than half were on the LNWR and the second largest total, 138, belonged to the GWR. Not all these early designs were intended for express passenger trains and not all designs were successful, but the type was to multiply, and modellers of the post-1923 era, and in particular the post-1948 period, should be aware of the role that the 4-6-0 played in working express passenger, ordinary passenger, mail, parcels and express freight trains. In their final years they could be found on virtually every class of train, but that was more about the rundown of the steam railway, as diesels were introduced, than their suitability for, say, ballast train duties!

Left: The BR 2-6-4T was a development of the final series of LMS passenger tank engines of the same wheel arrangement. A number were used on the Southern Region and this picture of No 80015 illustrates one hauling an 'Ordinary' passenger train. *S. C. Nash*

Below left: The GWR's 4-6-0 classes, which began to appear during the early years of the 20th century, were in advance of what was being built elsewhere in Great Britain for express passenger work. This picture, taken at Hereford on 8 May 1953, shows 'Saint' class No 2937 on an 'Ordinary' passenger train. To the left is 2-6-0 No 7308, which appears to be on station pilot duties. *T. J. Edgington*

Bottom left: Running as British Railways No 30829, this picture of an ex-Southern Railway 'S15' 4-6-0, built in 1927 and withdrawn in 1963, was taken at Basingstoke on 2 August 1958. *Author's collection*

Right, top to bottom:

The LMS Class 5s were probably the most successful of the mixed traffic 4-6-0s to be built by the 'Big Four'. This picture, taken at St Enoch on 6 May 1946, shows Nos 5213 and 5119 on the 1.45pm Glasgow to Carlisle express passenger train. *Author's collection*

The LNER 'B1s' were highly successful mixed traffic locomotives; they were also employed on express passenger work, although it is doubtful if the gross weight of this train exceeds 150 tons. Construction of 'B1s' continued after Nationalisation, and No 61392 was one of those that did not enter service until 1951. It is interesting to see that although this locomotive is equipped with electric headlamps, it has to carry two oil lamps to denote the class of train during the hours of daylight. *Author's collection*

British Railways' development of the Class 5 was a series of Standard engines numbered in the 73xxx series, and this picture, taken at Chorlton on 5 May 1951, shows No 73000 on the 4.10pm Derby to Manchester Central 'Ordinary' passenger train. *J. Davenport*

If there is one locomotive that I would always associate with David Jenkinson it would be 'Royal Scot' No 6170 *British Legion*. When I made the first of many visits to his home I saw the original Marthwaite EM layout and he had a model of 6170 at work on the line. I recall asking him what one of the most modern LMS passenger engines was doing on an obscure branch line in Yorkshire; his reply was most convincing! This picture shows his 7mm-scale model at the head of the Royal Train; note the headcode, His Majesty is in the train. *Tony Wright*

This is another picture of 'Claughton' No 6018 seen here leaving the tunnel at Marthwaite and passing the connection to the quarry that was one of the final additions to be made to the layout before David died. *Tony Wright*

Above: Horwich Mogul No 13004 at the head of the 'Dalesman' (note the express passenger train headcode) entering Kendal Castle station with the side of Kendal Castle engine shed and the steps to the signalbox just visible to the left of the picture. *Tony Wright*

Right: A GWR 2-6-0 has already been seen at Hereford, but here is another, No 6360, working a football excursion from Swindon on 23 February 1952. Almost all classes of Moguls were good mixed traffic engines, but this picture is particularly interesting. The train is arriving at Luton on the former Midland Railway London-Bedford line, and will have travelled from Swindon to Acton, then over the old Midland line to Brent, where it would have joined the Midland main line. *Author's collection*

Before we consider the final design of express passenger locomotive, the 4-6-2, we should note that the 2-6-0 or Mogul also played an important part in express passenger train working. Although not used for the most important work, 2-6-0s were frequently required to work specials and excursions under express headlamps. All of the 'Big Four' companies had good designs of 2-6-0, and I personally have a soft spot for them; the first express passenger train that I ever worked was with a Horwich Mogul from Birmingham to Sheffield, a splendid trip. This type, in power class 2, was introduced by the LMS in 1946 for use on branch lines and for secondary traffic, and as such they are well suited for the post-1948 branch-line modeller.

The 4-6-2, or Pacific, wheel arrangement represented the ultimate British express passenger locomotive. There were a few other experimental designs of locomotive intended for express passenger work, but their success varied and as far as this work is concerned they need not be considered. However, one wheel

Left: Although the Pacifics were normally associated with main-line express passenger trains, the LNER also used 2-6-2s, mixed traffic locomotives. A less onerous duty was to work 'Ordinary' passenger trains, in this instance comprising five carriages. This picture of 'V2' No 4830 was taken in March 1948 from Staverton Road signalbox on the former Great Central London Extension, a location that could provide inspiration for scenic modellers. *J. A. G. H. Coltas*

Top: The Stanier 'Coronation' 4-6-2s were splendid machines and this picture of No 46221 at Stafford on the Up 'Royal Scot' has been included to ensure that they are represented in this section of the book. One of the first batch to be built, *Queen Elizabeth* entered service as a streamlined locomotive, but by the time that this early British Railways-period picture was taken the streamlined casing had been removed.
H. Gordon Tidey

Above: Although the BR Class 6 4-6-2s were overshadowed by the larger and more numerous Class 7 'Britannias', I felt that this atmospheric picture could represent the final design of 4-6-2 to enter service in Great Britain. Photographed when approaching Lostock Junction, No 72002 *Clan Campbell* on the 9.30am Manchester Victoria to Glasgow train makes a magnificent sight.
J. Davenport

arrangement that was used very successfully by the LNER, but which did not appear on any of the other 'Big Four' systems in this form, was the 2-6-2 mixed traffic tender engine, such as the famous *Green Arrow* of the 'V2' class. As regards the Pacifics, with one exception there were none on the GWR until after Nationalisation, when the British Railways 'Britannia' class entered service. The Southern Railway was the last of the 'Big Four' to introduce this wheel arrangement, but in a few short years it produced a considerable number. The LMS built two types of 4-6-2, confined to a limited number of routes, leaving the LNER as the major user of this type in Great Britain.

I have always felt that unless you are modelling the final years of steam, when 4-6-2s were employed on all manner of trains as steam was run down and the change-over to diesel power continued, they should really be used to work express passenger trains with about 15 coaches, yet this length of train requires more space than many of us have available. For this reason many modellers build branch lines, so I would like to close this chapter by showing how the motive power changed over the years on one British country branch line.

The line I have chosen is not really typical — in fact it is rather unusual — but it embodies features and aspects that could be found on many British branch lines and which could be incorporated into models of this type of railway. The line from Barnt Green to Ashchurch, approximately 34 miles long, was a fascinating length of railway, mostly single track with passing loops, but with a double-track section at the southern end.

The passenger service was really three separate services. One treated the branch as a through line running from the major centre at Birmingham to the end of the branch at Ashchurch, although some services terminated at Evesham, where at one time there was an engine shed; even after the shed closed men were out-stationed at Evesham, where there was also a turntable and engine servicing facilities. Other passenger trains ran over only part of the branch before they terminated. At the north end of the line there was a service between Birmingham and Redditch, which the LMS would describe as 'residential', worked by 'turn-back trains'. Unlike the southern end of the line this section was fairly busy. Although the railway was double track at the southern end, that section was a country branch that ran through rural areas and did not serve any major centres of population. The passenger service was generally from Ashchurch to Evesham, although some trains terminated elsewhere.

I said that the branch was somewhat unusual, and at Broom there was a junction with the S&MJR, whose line allowed the Midland and later the LMS to run banana trains and other traffic to and from London and Bristol in competition with the GWR, while at Alcester the GWR had running powers into the Midland station. The GWR also had a small engine shed close to the Midland station. Until the passenger service over the S&MJR line was withdrawn there were

connecting services at Broom with both Up and Down Midland trains. This meant that it was possible to have three passenger trains at the same time at a single-line station that offered no more than a single island platform. I have always felt that the full-size railway could offer more remarkable operating features than modellers could ever invent!

The locomotives used on the passenger services changed over the years and in this respect the line was typical of British practice. Let us consider each section in turn, beginning with the Birmingham to Redditch trains. At first 2-4-0 tender engines worked these trains and there was a turntable at the small engine shed, but following the introduction of 0-4-4T engines for this work it was removed. These tank engines ran the passenger trains, 0-4-4Ts and 0-6-4Ts during the Midland and early LMS years, then later 2-6-2Ts and 2-6-4Ts.

At the southern end of the line the wheel arrangements changed little. At first there were again 2-4-0 tender engines, and probably 0-6-0 goods engines, but by the 1880s 0-4-4Ts, which remained in use into the British Railways era, were used on both passenger and goods workings, although in the final years Class 3F 0-6-0 tank engines replaced them.

The through services were in the hands of 2-4-0 and 0-6-0 tender engines, then came the 0-4-4Ts and 0-6-4Ts, followed by Class 2P 4-4-0s displaced from main-line work. In due course larger 2-6-2 and 2-6-4 tank engines were employed; then in the final years Class 4MT 2-6-0s were used. Although they were tender engines, they were ideal for this class of work, having the advantage of being able to carry more coal and water than a Class 4 tank engine; they were also fitted with tender cabs, which meant they could comfortably run tender-first and did not need to be turned. Further details, including signalling, track plans and timetables, will be found in my book on the line, listed in the Bibliography.

I have mentioned the use of 0-6-0 goods engines for passenger work, and while this was common practice during the pre-Grouping era, it also continued into the British Railways period, when 0-6-0s were regularly employed to work passenger trains throughout the British Isles. In some respects this was regular practice on branch lines, which helps to explain why turntables were found at some unexpected locations — the Board of Trade did not like passenger trains to be worked tender-first. A more demanding use of this type of locomotive was on excursion or special trains, when quite heavy trains would be taken. To list all the classes of 0-6-0s that could be used on a model could be lengthy, so some pictures have been included; the only requirement would be vacuum or Westinghouse brakes on the locomotive and steam heating during the time when this was an operating requirement.

In presenting this rather brief summary, no distinction has been made between inside-cylinder and outside-cylinder arrangements or compound engines, and although I have mentioned the Whyte notation, I have not explained what it was. Frederick Methvan Whyte was a Dutchman employed as a mechanical engineer on the New York Central Railroad. In about 1899 he devised what became the system used in the USA, United Kingdom and some Commonwealth countries. Prior to the adoption of the simple use of wheel arrangement to classify a locomotive, all manner of descriptions were used. For example, an 0-6-0T might be described as a 'six wheels coupled side tank goods engine', and an 0-4-4T as a 'four wheels coupled bogie passenger tank engine'. In my research into Derby Locomotive Works records I have noted the use of pre-Whyte descriptions as late as about 1930, so clearly old habits died hard. While I think that the pre-Whyte descriptions are rather delightful, I freely admit that they are not ideal and that his simple notations are more easily understood.

Left: It was not unusual to use 0-6-0s on passenger trains and this practice continued almost throughout the history of steam traction. I have selected three examples, one pre-1923, one during the Grouping period, and one post-1948. In the first, we see North Staffordshire Railway No 15A at Derby on a passenger train to Stoke-on-Trent; the NSR enjoyed running powers into the Midland Railway's Derby station. *C. H. Eden*

Top: The Grouping period is represented by this picture of ex-Midland Railway No 3096, photographed on 27 March 1937 at Kettering prior to working an 'Ordinary' passenger train to Cambridge. *H. F. Wheeller collection*

Above: LNER Class 'J39', now running as BR No 64838, is an example of the use of 0-6-0s to work passenger trains during the British Railways era. The train is running with an express train headcode and is a Derby Friargate to Skegness special, photographed near Breadsall on 15 July 1951. *R. J. Buckley*

Chapter Five

Passenger Stations

The question of stations and passenger traffic is rather like the proverbial 'chicken and egg' — which came first? Fortunately, with railways it was almost always the traffic potential that determined both the location and size of the station. However, it is worth noting that when Euston, one of the major stations in Great Britain, was completed in 1837 as the first main-line railway terminus in London it had but two platforms, yet by 1892 the number had grown to 15. The reverse could also apply, of course, as traffic was lost, generally to competition from road, tramways, buses and later cars, when a station would become too large or too well-equipped for the reduced level of traffic using it. At first it would assume an air of neglect, then later would come the inevitable closure. Therefore modellers of the post-1950 era should be mindful that there was little investment by British Railways in declining assets, and often an air of decay and neglect should be seen on models depicting stations during this period.

The full-size railways often used words to describe parts of the system that are either not used by modellers, or have different meanings when applied to models. In this work I have generally tried to use descriptions from the prototype railway, and will illustrate what I mean by the use of the word 'terminal'. When used for railway purposes it refers to both ends of a journey by rail, whereas modellers use it to describe a station at the end of the line. In a railway sense any station could be a terminal, but wherever possible the station was placed in the centre of the district it served.

In the early days of the steam railway the attention of the railway companies was mostly directed towards the carriage of goods and minerals; it was only later that the importance of passenger traffic began to be realised. A railway station represented a considerable outlay of capital for the company, and although there were occasions when one was re-sited, this was not common and enlargement was the more usual solution to meet the needs of increased traffic.

Below: Euston is one of the most important stations in the United Kingdom and has the distinction of being the first main-line railway terminus to open in London. Therefore it seems to me that our review of passenger stations should begin with this Edwardian view. The absence of people suggests a posed picture, but that does not detract from the atmosphere of this famous railway station. *Author's collection*

Right: From Euston we move to Wirksworth in Derbyshire to look at a country station in about 1905. There is a reasonable amount of traffic on the platform — milk churns, hampers and wicker baskets waiting to be loaded on to the next train, while others have arrived and will be taken away by road. *Author's collection*

Below right: This 1950s photograph of Bletchley presents a different picture. I would think that the various bicycles and motorcycles on the platform belong to railwaymen working at the station, but there appears to be some traffic on the left-hand platform, together with a number of platform trolleys. *Lens of Sutton*

Above: This is one of my favourite pictures. Taken at Long Eaton station, near Nottingham, on 18 September 1911, it has been included to illustrate a number of station features. Although there is a barrow crossing between the platforms, this is not for passengers — note the two signs that state that passengers must use the bridge. The crossing was only for railway staff, probably with barrows. The ramps at the end of the platforms — steps were not allowed by the Board of Trade — can also be seen. The arrangement of the level crossing and adjacent signalbox was commonplace on all British railway companies. The stop signals for both the Up and Down line protecting the level crossing were, of course, also a requirement. *Author's collection*

Left: The romance of the Royal Mail train is now a thing of the past, and scenes like this no longer form part of the railway scene. It appears to be about 10pm and Class 5 No 44877 is at the head of a mail train with mailbags being loaded and unloaded by railway and Post Office staff.
Mile Post 92½/A. W. V. Mace collection

Right: The absence of any road vehicle suggests that this is a posed picture, but at least it does allow a clear view of the type of railway signs and advertising that could be seen at a major station, in this case Leeds in 1914. *Author's collection*

Therefore modellers should be aware that there is potential for building models of cramped station layouts as well as those that suggest they have just been enlarged.

Before we look at stations by type we should perhaps consider them from the standpoint of the full-size railways and try to see what we can learn when planning a model that is not based upon an actual location. In *Railway Operation* I examined some of the legislation introduced over the years that applied to railways. Although the subject is very wide, I will summarise what might be useful to modellers as far as stations are concerned so

that they can ensure they do not break the rules. This information has been taken from a Board of Trade document dated 1896. However, I must point out that the legislation was not retrospective and certain features that applied to older stations remained and were altered only if work was undertaken by the railway company and a new inspection by the Board of Trade, or later, the Ministry of Transport was required.

The Board stipulated that at terminal stations a double line of railway must not end as a single line (a 'double line of railway' should not be confused with a single line that has a run-

Below: In the days before TV advertising, very considerable use was made of poster boards, and this picture, taken close to an entrance to Birmingham New Street station, shows a number of features that will be of interest to modellers: the rather ornate street lamp, the cobblestones or setts, the late-1920s dress of the pedestrians, and of course the posters, both railway and commercial. *Author's collection*

round loop at the terminal end). In the case of double lines or of passing places on single lines, each line should have its own platform, and platforms were to be continuous and not less than 6ft wide for stations of small traffic, and not less than 12ft wide for important stations.

The descents at the ends of the stations should be by ramps and not by steps. Pillars for

the support of roofs and other fixed works were to be not less than 6ft from the edge of a platform. The height of the platform above rail level was to be 3ft, save under exceptional circumstances, and in no case should be less than 2ft 6in. The edge of the platform should overhang not less than 12in, and as little space as possible was to be left between the edge of a platform and the footboards of carriages.

Shelters were to be provided on every platform, and conveniences where necessary. Names of stations must be shown on boards and on the platform lamps. Footbridges or subways must be provided for passengers to cross the railway at all exchange points and other important stations. Staircases or ramps leading to or from platforms should at no point be narrower than at the top, and the available width was in no case to be contracted by any erection or boxed obstructions whatever below the top. A clock was to be provided at every station, in some conspicuous position visible from the platforms.

Finally there was an interesting requirement for turntables. Engine turntables of sufficient diameter to enable the longest engines and tenders in use on the line to be turned without being uncoupled were to be erected at terminal stations and at junctions at which engines required to be turned, except in cases of short lines not exceeding 15 miles in length, where stations were not at a greater distance than

Far left: This posed 19th-century picture, taken before the London, Chatham & Dover Railway combined with the South Eastern Railway, has been included to show a porter with a trunk on a platform barrow. Are they attempting to load this into a compartment? A piece of luggage this size would normally be carried in the brake-van. However, the picture is useful in so far that it reminds us that, other than unmanned halts, we should include a complement of barrows and trolleys at all stations. *Greenwich Library*

Left: One form of sign to be seen at some railway stations was the finger-board pointing to the platform from which the train that was described by the board would depart, as well as giving the time of departure. This example was photographed at Trent on the north side of the station. *M. S. Cross*

Below left: Although this picture at Derby was originally taken to show the new station lighting, it also provides readers with a number of railway signs that could be seen at many stations. Note the two scissor crossovers on both sides of the platform. They enabled trains and carriages to be shunted as described on page 32. *Author's collection*

3 miles apart and the railway company gave an undertaking to stop all trains at all stations.

So much for the rules — now to the function. The object of a passenger station is to provide the means whereby a passenger or parcel can get from the road to the train or vice versa. Costs were always a major consideration, and the further passengers had to walk from the point of entry to where they could join the train, the greater the cost to the railway company in terms of maintenance, staffing and lighting, to say nothing of the original cost of building. The same principles applied to parcels and similar traffic that was carried by passenger train. The railway companies tried to ensure that there was, as far as possible, free movement for the flows of traffic, so modellers designing station layouts should try to follow this approach.

Other forms of traffic passed through passenger stations besides passengers; I have mentioned parcels, a general railway term, but they could be either accompanied passengers' luggage or unaccompanied traffic such as birds and livestock, perishable traffic, Post Office mails, etc, almost all of which would be taken to the train by platform trolleys or barrows of various types. Examples of these items add atmosphere to models of stations. At some stations loading docks were provided to deal with more bulky items; such docks were side-loading for traffic that could be dealt with in that way and end-loading for wheeled vehicles. The traffic using docks at passenger stations would include horseboxes, motor car vans and theatrical trucks; where possible a separate road entrance for these loading docks was provided to avoid interfering with passenger traffic.

With the possible exception of dock or harbour stations, passengers would arrive at the station by some form of road transport or on foot. Therefore adequate road access was necessary and, other than at the smaller type of station, it was usual to arrange for taxis and cars to be able to arrive, unload and move on without fouling the approach of other vehicles. Unless they had advance tickets, passengers then proceeded to the booking office — some large stations had more than one — and those passengers with luggage would find porters on hand; handbarrows and trolleys would be needed to move any heavy luggage. At the station entrance it was normal to display notices and timetables, and these should be provided on your model.

Most passengers arrive before the trains, so seats would be found at all stations; even the smallest halt would usually have one, although there were exceptions. Waiting rooms and lavatories would also be provided at the majority of stations, and some would have refreshment rooms. We must not overlook the various staff facilities, which would include a porters' room, lamp room, parcels office and station master's office. Common to all stations would be lighting, whether oil, gas or electric. Depending upon the size of the station there might be weighing machines, pillar boxes or wall boxes to post mail, telephone call boxes — but not always GPO standard kiosks — telegraph offices, bookstalls, stalls for tobacco, fruit and sweets, and automatic vending machines for cigarettes or chocolate.

Signs are an important part of every station and, as specified by the Board of Trade above, it was essential that the name of the station should be prominently displayed to passengers on arriving trains. Other signs would depend upon the facilities at the station, but might include 'Booking Office', 'Left Luggage Office', 'Waiting Room', 'Enquiry Office', 'Refreshment Room', and signs indicating lavatories and exits, as well as platform number boards and trespass signs. Train Departure Indicators were used at larger stations, and at some various forms of indicator boards were also used on the platforms. Finally, we must not forget the all-important station clock.

It is not uncommon on models to find station pilots where none would exist if the station was a real place. The railways took the view that, wherever possible, the shunting of passenger coaches should be undertaken either by the train's own engine or by another during intervals between its own workings, and thus such movements would be part of the engine work diagram. Where it was necessary to roster a shunting engine to work at a passenger station every effort would be made to ensure that it was gainfully employed. At some stations the pilot was a large passenger engine, which was there to replace a failed main-line locomotive should the need arise, but if this was not the case an 0-6-0T or similar locomotive fitted with automatic brakes would be employed.

Station pilots bring us to the question of locomotive facilities at stations, and the answer is that generally there were none. However, the most common feature to be found would have been water columns to enable locomotives to take on supplies of water. There were various rules about the position of water columns; one was that they should be at the end of a platform or through road with sufficient clearance to enable the engine to come to a stand at the stop signal and at the same time to make use of the water column. When trains were double-headed and both engines desired to take water, unless two water columns were provided — and this was found only at stations where double-heading was regular practice — it was often necessary for the stop signal to be cleared so that after the first engine had taken water it could draw ahead to enable the second to come alongside the water column.

Where engine facilities were provided, as at a major station, junction or terminal, they might comprise a turntable and engine pits for inspection purposes or raking out the ashpan. What was less common was any coaling facility; out-and-back workings would more likely be made on the basis that the locomotive would take on enough coal at the home shed for the round trip and the coal for the return trip would be brought forward from the rear of the tender while standing at the engine sidings. The use of this servicing arrangement avoided the need for light engine movements between station and engine shed and therefore reduced line occupation. Although it was desirable to have both the engine shed and carriage sidings close to a major station, in particular a terminal, this was not always possible, so these engine sidings acted as a form of subsidiary shed for locomotives between diagrammed workings.

When the carriage sheds and engine sheds were not close to a major station, locomotives would have to run from the engine shed to the carriage sidings, couple to the empty stock, then run into the station. It saved time if, upon arrival, all that had to be done was to change the locomotive headlamp code from empty stock to passenger, but sometimes the locomotive would have to run round the train and work back in the direction of the carriage sidings. In these circumstances, if the locomotive was a tender engine the empty stock working would have been made tender-first.

I do not ever recall seeing a model of either carriage sidings or a carriage shed, perhaps with cleaning facilities. Sometimes the work of carriage cleaning was done in the open; at other places it was more like a modern car-washing plant. The only article about this subject known to me is in *Midland Record 18* (see the Bibliography). As well as holding complete sets of coaches, some carriage sidings would also have spare vehicles that could be used for strengthening purposes as described in Chapter 1.

'Platforming' is a railway term used to describe the work and organisation on the station platform. In a model this would include the train driver stopping so that the luggage or parcels van would be close to the trolleys and barrows that

Right: Many modellers make great use of station pilots rather than using, as the railway companies often did, train engines for shunting purposes. I have selected three examples to show station pilots at work; all were taken post-1948 and show engines displaying the headlamp code of one lamp over each buffer at both ends. Former Midland 0-4-4T No 1396, now running as British Railways No 58076, was photographed at Sheffield Midland station in April 1952 when working as station pilot. It is standing on one of the centre roads and is coupled to a pair of milk tanks, but it is not possible to say if they are about to be attached to a train or if they have just been detached.
Midland Railway Trust

Centre right: Built in 1913, ex-North British Railway Class C15 4-4-2T No 67474 was photographed in February 1953 when coupled to an ex-LMS passenger brake-van. Note again the lamps above each buffer, front and back.
Author's collection

Below right:
Photographed at Carlisle on 4 June 1960, the station pilot, an ex-Midland Railway Class 3F carrying the BR number 43240, is standing in the centre road at the station. At major provincial stations it was usual to have one or two roads or sidings between the platform lines where empty stock or engines could stand 'out of the way', to use the railway expression. As can be seen, a station pilot could be either a tender or tank engine, but where there was a possibility that it might be required to assist trains, it was usual for it to be a passenger tender locomotive.
D. F. Tee

were loaded with parcels for the train or waiting to be loaded from the train. On the full-size railway this was not difficult to arrange; the carriage marshalling diagrams would set out the train formation and past experience would dictate what would happen. To underline this point it is worth looking at pictures of trains at passenger stations and you will see that the engine usually has come to a halt at the same place each time. Railway work was repetitive — the same thing was done the same way each time. In other words, having found the best way to do something, the method was not changed.

One feature of platforming that may appeal to space-starved modellers is the practice of 'drawing up'. Trains were, and sometimes still are, scheduled to call at stations where the platform was not long enough to accommodate the entire train. Two options were available: the first was to stop with the engine just beyond the end of the platform so that passengers could alight from the front of the train, then 'draw up' the train to bring the rear coaches alongside the platform; the alternative was to ensure that there were no passengers in the front coaches for the stations where the train would have to draw forward, so that the engine and these coaches could overrun the platform. The latter course was preferred as it saved time, and would make an interesting feature on a model of a station with short platforms and long trains.

In the LMS training manual *Passenger Station Working*, the company classified passengers under four headings, explaining their travelling needs: 'Residential', 'Business', 'Non-Business' and 'Excursion'. Although much of what was written is not relevant to modellers, the question of the stock that would be used by these various classes of passenger and the stations they travelled to and from is most important.

In 1938 'Residential' passengers were what today we would describe as commuters, season ticket holders or daily travellers. They did not require luggage vans to be part of the train and they travelled in fixed formations of carriages that were rarely strengthened or divided. 'Business' travellers generally used main-line trains and expected a higher level of attention, which meant restaurant cars, and sleeping carriages on some overnight trains. 'Non-business' travellers were considered as being infrequent, and although the manual does not say so, this class of traveller might use any category of train.

The final category was the 'excursion' or cheap ticket holder. Almost from the beginning of railway history excursion trains have been part of the railway scene, yet they are rarely if ever modelled. I can only assume that this is because today variable-price tickets are available for most trains on the privatised railway system and separate excursion trains went out of favour many years ago. At one time it was not uncommon for the railway companies to retain old stock for excursion purposes and for some stock to be used only a few times each year. I understand that at times some of these infrequently used sets did not have any lighting in the compartments.

What the LMS manual did not describe was workmen's and staff trains. The former category included trains to carry miners — or, as they were often described, 'colliers' — and these were the most common, although some large works or factories often generated the need for special trains to carry their employees to and from their place of work. Although the distance run was quite short and the fares low, the revenue would be welcomed by the railway company. Staff trains were also run to carry railway employees, and there are a number of examples of stations that were opened for this purpose.

The LMS manual also sets out five classes of station, stating that 'the type of station, there-

I have mentioned that at many stations water cranes or columns were placed at the end of the platforms, and this picture of Hooton shows this feature rather well. Three columns can be seen, together with their frost fires, which were kept alight during cold weather whenever there was a possibility of the water freezing. This type of column was described by the LMS as a 'standpipe'. Both locomotives are LMS Stanier Class 3 2-6-2Ts, now in British Railways ownership as Nos 40110 and 40135, on Birkenhead and West Kirby trains. *Mile Post 92½/A. W. V. Mace collection*

fore, in relation to the traffic handled, is of great importance'. While the characteristics of most stations vary, there were broadly five classes: halts, roadside or country stations, large suburban stations, large through provincial stations, and terminal stations. To this list I would add dock or harbour stations, used only in connection with passengers arriving by or continuing their journey by ship (these are, of course, a form of terminal station). Under the heading of halts one could also include workmen's and colliers' halts, which were not advertised in the public timetables, and those used by railway staff or during wartime by workers engaged on Government work. The omission of 'junction stations' as a category is, in my view, surprising, but clearly the LMS did not consider that a separate classification was required. Neither did the LMS manual include interchange platforms; these were not always staffed and usually did not have road access, although in some cases there were footpaths. Examples include Dovey Junction on the Cambrian Railways, Bala Junction (GWR), Roudham Junction Halt (GER), Cairnie Junction (GNoSR), and Halehouse (GSWR).

Left: Signalboxes at roadside stations were often placed on the platforms, when they would usually be conventional signalboxes built in accordance with the owning company's practice. At major provincial stations, boxes that were within the station area were sometimes very different, as this picture of the West Signal Box at Leicester illustrates. *Author's collection*

Above: Some stations did not have a conventional signalbox. For example, on a single line there might be stations that were not block posts, which therefore had no need of one. At others the 'signalbox' was on the platform and took the form of a ground frame or, as it is sometimes called, a stage, with the instruments close by. This example was at Hykeham on the old Midland line between Lincoln and Newark. *Author's collection*

The 1938 LMS manual also contains a reference to the historical development of the company's stations, a statement that no doubt applied to all other major British railway companies: 'In a large number of cases our stations, especially the larger ones, have serious disadvantages from an accommodation and layout point of view, and would have been constructed differently had it been possible originally to forecast the likely development of traffic.' This is very helpful to space-starved modellers and enables them to justify a cramped and far from ideal arrangement at a station, provided the basic rules about signalling and track formation are not broken; both subjects are considered at length in *Railway Operation for the Modeller*. In other words, although the layout was not ideal and improvements were planned, the railway company had to get Board of Trade — later Ministry of Transport — approval for any alterations before they could be used on a permanent basis for passenger trains.

Let us therefore look at the various types of station in more detail, with photographs and plans. Some of the plans are actual locations and are identified, while others, although based upon real places, are included as 'typical examples'. I felt that this was the best way to show different locations that might be found on any of the major British railway companies' lines. In a number of cases it proved difficult to separate the passenger and goods facilities; depending on the type of station, the goods arrangements have either been shown in full or reference made to where they could be placed. In each example it is for you the modeller to decide how best the plans could be adapted to suit your purpose, and to signal them in accordance with the general principles set out in *Railway Operation for the Modeller*. To have included full prototype signalling arrangements would have been prohibitively complex, and I feel that the question of signalling, and the changes that were made over the years, should be considered as a separate subject.

Halts and Unadvertised Halts for Workmen and Colliers

These were small stations that could be used either by the public, and were therefore advertised in the public timetable, or were unadvertised halts for workers. On a single line one platform would suffice, but on double-track lines they were usually made with a platform for each line. At best the accommodation was usually no more than a simple shelter, and some had nothing at all. Staff levels were minimal, if they existed at all, although if there was a manned level crossing near the halt then at least the crossing-keeper, who was employed by the railway company, would be to hand.

Simplicity was the keynote for this class of

station, and it was not uncommon for stations of this type, in particular the workmen's halts, to have no more than a fence at the rear of the platform and some lights, with no shelter being provided. Tickets were issued on the train by the guard, so vestibule stock was used, or a

single railmotor. Platform heights varied, and when they were low access to the train was by either fixed or collapsible steps.

The GWR also had a slightly higher grade of halt, known as a 'Platform', staffed by a Grade 1 Porter.

Right top to bottom:
The short branch from Harpenden to Hemel Hempstead terminated at Heath Park Halt, seen in this 1934 view looking towards Harpenden. Note the simple wooden platform with a fence to the rear, two gas lamps and no form of shelter for passengers. Note also the form of checkrail where the line passes over the two roads, one in the foreground and the other beyond the end of the platform.
Author's collection

We conclude this section with a workmen's station that I knew well some 50 years ago. Longbridge, on the Halesowen Joint line (GWR & LMS [Midland]), only handled traffic for the Austin Motor Company and the passenger trains were for workmen employed at the plant. The two trains are the 7.8am from Saltley (left), headed by 2-6-4T No 42337, and a workmen's train from Old Hill hauled by 0-6-0T No 7428.
T. J. Edgington

The simplest arrangement for a halt was on a single line with a platform and waiting shelter. This class of halt was built during the 1920s/30s to serve new housing estates. An example of a rather more ornate halt, built prior to the Great War for this class of traffic, will be found in my book on the LT&SR. Access varied: if the halt was serving a new housing estate, it might be in the middle of the countryside with little more than a footpath to it. It might be in a cutting or on an embankment, accessed from an adjacent road underbridge (over the railway) or overbridge (under the railway); readers may find *Railway Archive No 4* and L. V. Wood's *Bridges For Modellers* (see the Bibliography) helpful in understanding this aspect of engineering and the correct terms to use. The same arrangement of a single platform would apply if it was a non-advertised workmen's halt — the difference would be the surroundings. If it was a colliers' halt, the colliery would not be far away, or it could be some form of large industrial undertaking.

Not all halts were on single lines — examples on double-track lines were quite common. Normally passengers would approach from one side, and there would be a foot crossing connecting the platform ends. There might also be waiting shelters on both platforms, and my previous remarks regarding access also apply here.

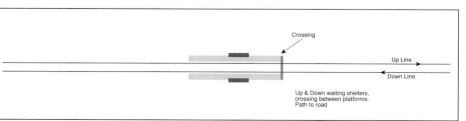

Roadside or Country Stations

This was undoubtedly the largest group, ranging from small stations on single-line branches, with or without a passing loop, to stations on multi-track lines. The siding accommodation could consist of nothing at all, a single siding, or extensive goods facilities. Examples of roadside stations of various sizes are shown in the accompanying illustrations and plans.

Although I have shown junction stations as a separate category, the railway companies would have classified some junction stations under this heading.

I have also been unsure how detailed to make the signalling information. Much would depend upon the traffic and track layout in the area of the station. Therefore I have taken the view that readers could refer to the principles set out in *Railway Operation for the Modeller* and that maybe the question of signalling could be a separate subject.

Top to bottom:
Rushden station was on the Higham Ferrers branch in Northamptonshire and this picture shows a train from Higham Ferrers to Wellingborough. Although the locomotive is motor-fitted it is pulling the train, which does not appear to consist of motor-fitted vehicles. Note the reasonably sized goods yard, underlining the fact that small stations on single lines do not have to have small goods yards. *H. F. Wheeller*

Annan, on the Caledonian Railway branch from Kirtlebridge, was renamed Annan Shawhill by the LMS in 1924. This LMS-period view provides another example of a small country station on a single line. There are a number of milk churns on the platform, traffic that would be expected in a country district. The small goods yard can be seen in the distance, partly hidden by the steam from the unidentified ex-Caledonian 0-4-4T engine. *Author's collection*

Brynamman West was the old GWR station on the Garnant branch in South Wales. To avoid confusion with the nearby ex-Midland station at Brynamman, the word 'West' was added to the name in 1950. Beyond the bridge there was a junction where the old Midland and Great Western lines came together, both stations acting as terminals for passenger traffic, but freight could run over the lines of one company on to the other. Modellers have neglected the South Wales area, but there are numerous stations and, as we will see in the forthcoming book on freight operations, simple colliery lines that could be modelled. This picture was taken in July 1958, three years before the station closed. *Author's collection*

This undated view of Gilnockie (for Claygate) is looking towards the junction with the main line at Riddings. This old North British branch ran to the terminus at Langholm, and Gilnockie dealt with a variety of goods traffic in the small yard, part of which can be seen to the right. *Author's collection*

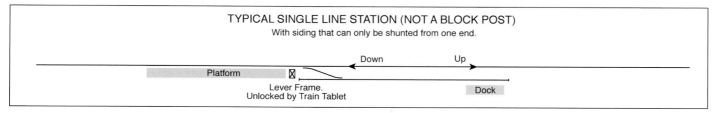

TYPICAL SINGLE LINE STATION (NOT A BLOCK POST)
With siding that can only be shunted from one end.

Down   Up

Platform

Lever Frame.
Unlocked by Train Tablet

Dock

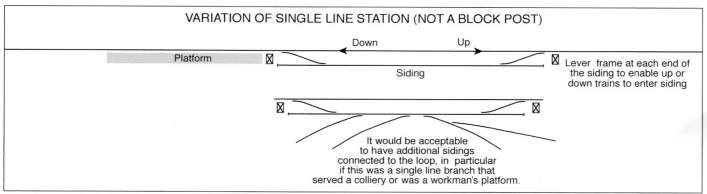

VARIATION OF SINGLE LINE STATION (NOT A BLOCK POST)

Down   Up

Platform

Siding

Lever frame at each end of
the siding to enable up or
down trains to enter siding

It would be acceptable
to have additional sidings
connected to the loop, in particular
if this was a single line branch that
served a colliery or was a workman's platform.

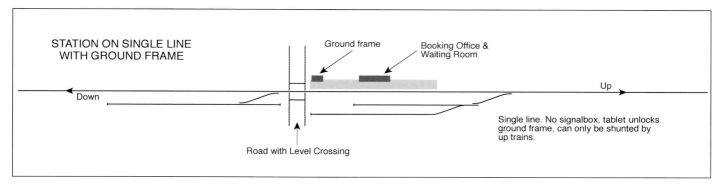

**STATION ON SINGLE LINE
WITH GROUND FRAME**

Ground frame

Booking Office &
Waiting Room

Up

Down

Road with Level Crossing

Single line. No signalbox, tablet unlocks
ground frame, can only be shunted by
up trains.

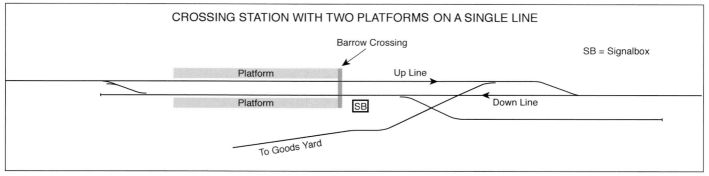

CROSSING STATION WITH TWO PLATFORMS ON A SINGLE LINE

Barrow Crossing

SB = Signalbox

Platform   Up Line

Platform   SB   Down Line

To Goods Yard

Top to bottom:
Not every station had a signalbox, which meant that not every station was a block post. This roadside station is little more than a halt, but there would probably be a small station building with a booking office and waiting rooms and possibly a porter's room — the facilities would depend upon the level of traffic. The goods siding can be entered only by trains travelling in the Down direction, and access would be gained by using the key or token that formed part of the single-line authority to unlock the lever frame.

In this variation it is possible for both Up and Down trains to set back into the siding, but otherwise the arrangements described in the previous plan also apply to this. Some stations on single lines had a number of sidings (see the accompanying photograph of Rushden), so an alternative arrangement is shown, with additional sidings connected to the loop.

Here is another small station on a single line, without a signalbox but equipped with a ground frame that could be unlocked with the train tablet or staff. There would

probably be signals to protect the level crossing, which would be worked from the ground frame. At this class of station there would be block instruments that might be by the frame, or more likely placed in the booking office. All passenger trains would probably stop here. An example of this arrangement will be found at Bethesda in *Railway Operation for the Modeller.*

Stations on single lines offer various choices when it comes to the question of layout. This example is a station that also serves as a crossing point, enabling two trains to pass one another. Note that where there is a junction between a single and a double line, the track plan is such that the entry to the passing loop at each end is straight, while the exit is curved. For this example I have shown a trailing connection from the Up line into the goods yard, which might be no more than a single siding — freight workings for this type of station will be described in the forthcoming book on freight operations. I would expect all passenger trains to stop at the station and, depending upon the circumstances, it would not be unreasonable to deal with a certain amount of passenger-rated parcels traffic.

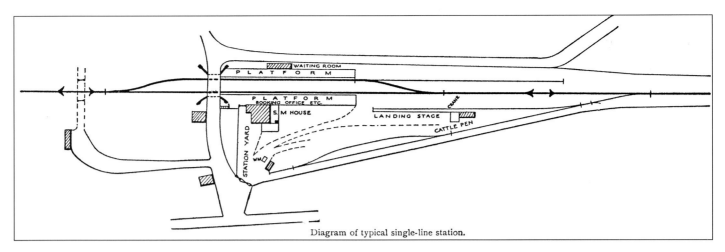

Diagram of typical single-line station.

Above: Here is another example of a single-line station with a passing loop. Although no signalbox was shown on the original plan, there could have been one at the landing stage end of the platform. If this was the case, the loop might need to be longer to allow two trains to pass. The plan as drawn shows the station to be on an embankment, with the station entrance at road level and the main buildings on the Down side of the line. The track layout is for a roadside station that has a lay-by on the Up side and a small goods yard on the Down. The track layout could also be used for a station where the approach was on the same level as the railway.

Centre right: While dealing with single lines, I felt that a picture of a light railway station should be included in this section, and this 15 August 1931 view shows the Kent & East Sussex Railway's Rolvenden station and locomotive shed. This type of railway fascinates many modellers, although I have always been drawn to main lines rather than light railways. Before road vehicles eroded their value for local transport, they had an important role to play, but by the 1920s they did not really have any future. *Author's collection*

Right: Evercreech New station should not be confused with Evercreech Junction, which was about 2 miles to the south. This north-facing picture, taken in June 1964, illustrates a country station with the signalbox and a small waiting shelter on the Up platform, and the main station building on the Down platform. No footbridge is provided; any passengers who wish to cross the line must use the barrow crossing. This was common practice at many similar stations, regardless of owning company. Entry to the small goods shed was by a trailing connection from the Down line, while to the left there was another siding and loading stage. To enable engines to run round their trains there was a trailing crossover to the south, behind the photographer. *Paul Cotterell*

Left: Some country or roadside stations were quite small, even though they were on major main lines. This picture of Monsal Dale, on the Rowsley and Buxton line, was taken in 1911 and shows a small country station. The signalbox is behind the photographer and the crossover has been set for the goods yard off to the right — normally the points would be set for through running. The goods yard was small, with a capacity for just seven wagons, while the lay-by siding could hold 45. Note that one platform has a timber surface while the other has been built in the traditional manner. Lighting is fairly minimal, only one platform seat can be seen, and passengers crossed the line by the barrow crossing. *Author's collection*

Centre Left: Desford was on the Leicester and Burton line. The first station was opened in 1832, but in 1848 a new station was built about 150 yards away to replace it. When the original station was built the platform was at a lower height than the required minimum that was later specified, but unless the station buildings were rebuilt the low-height platforms would have to remain. The solution was to increase the height of one platform and to extend the other as shown in this picture. This 1952 photograph illustrates a prototype that offers the modeller an interesting example of what actually happened, without the need to invent. The coaches of a train would always run alongside the platform extension, and passengers joining or leaving trains would have to walk from one to the other. There was a signalbox and level crossing behind the photographer. *Author's collection*

Below: The photographer is standing on the level crossing and facing north to take this picture of Coalville station, which was on the Leicester and Burton line and, as the name suggests, in a coal-mining district. It has been included to draw attention to the height of the signalbox. Tall signalboxes were more expensive to install and, I presume, to maintain, so they would be used only when it was necessary to increase the height in order to provide the signalman with a clear view. Beyond the platforms there was an engine shed, goods sidings and goods station; the only reason for placing the signalbox at the south end of the station was the level crossing. *Author's collection*

Above: Turvey station, on the MR's Bedford and Northampton line, was another example of a quiet country station. This 11 August 1959 picture shows 2-6-2T No 41329 propelling a motor train; the driver can just be glimpsed in the leading driving compartment. *Author's collection*

Below: St Columb Road, on the GWR's line between Newquay and Par, catered for all classes of freight traffic, although its passenger facilities appear to be somewhat limited. I presume that when this undated picture was taken there was a stopping freight train at the station, otherwise it is difficult to explain why there is a wagon standing at the platform. *Courtesy of John Jennison*

Right: The Great Eastern station at Dereham was on the Wymondham and Fakenham line and this 7 June 1952 picture shows the 12.50pm Wells to Norwich Thorpe 'Ordinary' passenger train headed by 4-4-0 No 62577. The main station buildings are to the left, where there is also a bay platform, while on the right the top of the goods shed can be seen. *Author's collection*

Left: The old North British Railway station at Hawick was on the line between Carlisle and Galashiels, and this south-facing photograph was taken in July 1967. The station was built on a curve with a fairly substantial footbridge connecting the two platforms, hence the need to build a tall signalbox to give the signalman a clear view. The ramp at the end of the platform is rather steep and there are some curious footholds to be seen. *Author's collection*

Right: This rather atmospheric picture was taken at Bulwell, on the Nottingham and Mansfield line, in March 1959. The 'Ordinary' passenger train, hauled by 2-6-2T No 40168, was probably a three-coach set comprising two Third Brakes and a Composite. There was a small goods yard here and the station signalbox can just be seen in the distance. *Author's collection*

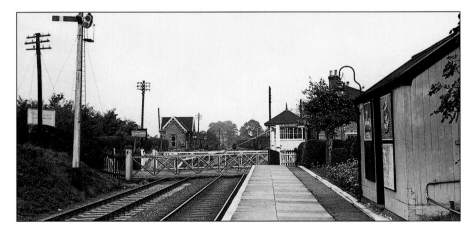

Top: The old Great Central station at Birdwell & Hoylake Common was a substantial brick-built structure with, I presume, the station master's house to the right. Although it was more common to build the dwelling for the station master away from the station, there are numerous examples where it was part of the establishment. *Author's collection*

Centre: Wellington station was on the Great Western line from Wolverhampton, and is the subject of a fine 4mm-scale model that was featured in *Railway Operation for the Modeller*. The station was used by both the GWR and LMS, although when this picture was taken in July 1950 it was all British Railways. To the left we can see one of the GWR's 2-6-2Ts, No 4406, which will work the 4.30pm to Much Wenlock, while the other locomotive is motor-fitted ex-LNWR 'Coal Tank' No 58904, due to work the 3.53pm to Coalport. *T. J. Edgington*

Above: Staggered platforms were not unusual at a station with a level crossing, and this picture of Countesthorpe on the Midland Counties Rugby branch, taken in 1952, has been included to illustrate this feature. *D. F. Tee*

Right top to bottom:
This typical roadside station could be on a slight embankment with the road approach to the station on the Down side of the line, where the main station buildings would be found, with just a waiting shelter on the Up platform. The connection between the platforms would be by a subway. An alternative would be an overbridge for passengers and a barrow crossing for staff with barrows and trolleys. Some passenger trains might pass through, with others stopping — it would depend upon the importance of the station. Only Up goods trains can access the sidings via the trailing points. The Up lay-by is used as a refuge siding to allow faster trains to pass slower traffic.

This plan shows a very common arrangement of station, and incorporates two variations of track layout. I have assumed that this station is on level ground with a footbridge and barrow crossing connecting the platforms, but there could be a subway, or the road access could be from a road passing over the railway with a footbridge to both platforms. The Up and Down sidings could be refuge sidings into which slow moving trains would be shunted to allow faster trains to overtake, or they could be used for traffic purposes. I think that it would be better to use them as the former, with one of them leading to the goods sidings, which we are assuming are on the Up side of the line. The trailing connection from the Down main line would enable a train to set back, while an Up train could set back through the crossover by the signalbox. If this arrangement was used, the Up siding would be part of the goods yard and only the Down siding would be used for refuge purposes.

In many respects an island platform had many advantages to offer, one being that buildings did not have to be duplicated, but the main problem was one of access. This example is a double-track station with a small goods yard on the Down side, which can be entered by trains travelling in either direction. The plan shows a low-level road approach to both the station and goods yard, but an alternative would be to have a bridge over the station and the entrance from this road. Care would need to be taken not to have the road entrance to the goods yard on a steep gradient.

End- and/or side-loading docks were a common feature of roadside stations, and this plan shows a track layout for a double-line station where the goods facilities could be anything from minimal to quite extensive. On the Up side there is a siding that, if it was long enough, could act as a refuge siding or lay-by, but if it was short it could be used to store wagons that had either been detached from an Up train or were waiting to be attached to one — for example, horse traffic that had been loaded at the side dock on the Down side of the station.

Staggered platforms are rarely modelled, probably because they require more space than a more conventional layout. There was always a reason for the arrangement, but sometimes with the passage of time it is not clear why it was done. In this example I have shown a barrow crossing between the platforms, but a road with a level crossing was not uncommon, and the platforms set on either side avoided a stopping train blocking the road longer than necessary. With a road level crossing the signalbox would be moved to be adjacent to it.

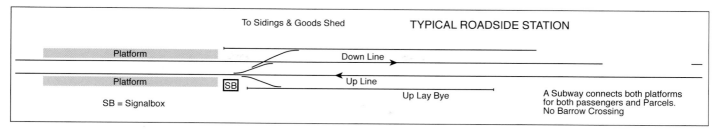

TYPICAL ROADSIDE STATION

To Sidings & Goods Shed

Platform

Down Line

Platform

SB

Up Line

SB = Signalbox

Up Lay Bye

A Subway connects both platforms for both passengers and Parcels. No Barrow Crossing

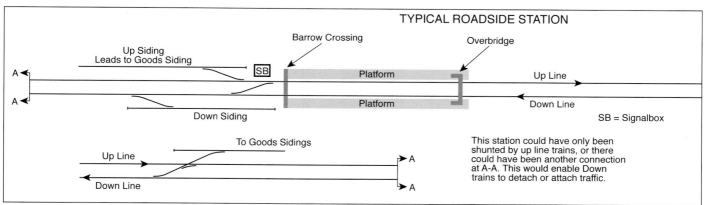

TYPICAL ROADSIDE STATION

Barrow Crossing

Overbridge

Up Siding
Leads to Goods Siding

SB

Platform

Up Line

A

A

Platform

Down Line

Down Siding

SB = Signalbox

To Goods Sidings

Up Line

A

Down Line

A

This station could have only been shunted by up line trains, or there could have been another connection at A-A. This would enable Down trains to detach or attach traffic.

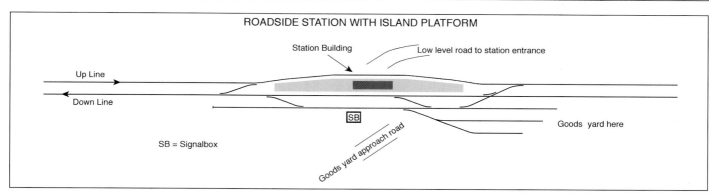

ROADSIDE STATION WITH ISLAND PLATFORM

Station Building

Low level road to station entrance

Up Line

Down Line

SB

Goods yard here

SB = Signalbox

Goods yard approach road

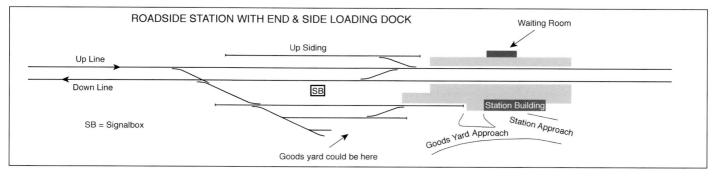

ROADSIDE STATION WITH END & SIDE LOADING DOCK

Waiting Room

Up Siding

Up Line

Down Line

SB

Station Building

SB = Signalbox

Station Approach

Goods Yard Approach

Goods yard could be here

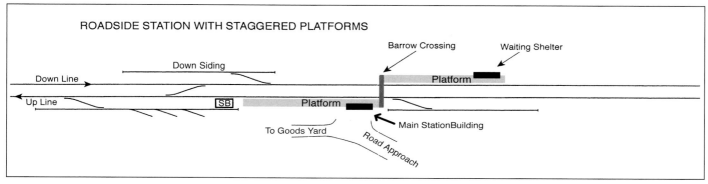

ROADSIDE STATION WITH STAGGERED PLATFORMS

Barrow Crossing

Waiting Shelter

Down Siding

Down Line

Platform

Up Line

SB

Platform

Main Station Building

To Goods Yard

Road Approach

Right: Elstree station, on the old Midland Railway London and Bedford line, is a good example of a station served by four platforms. This undated picture is looking south; the slow lines are to the left and the fast lines to the right, with the station signalbox behind the photographer. There was also a gasworks, to the left of the picture, with a rail connection to the north of the station. *Author's collection*

Below right: This undated picture, taken at Barnby Dun on the old Great Central Railway between Doncaster and Thorne, is rather curious. To the right of the picture we can see the signalbox, main station buildings and a rather short platform. The new island platform was built when the line was realigned and I assume that the old platform is no longer used. There are plenty of examples of stations that were modified over the years, and they offer creative modellers the opportunity to build something that is rather different. *Author's collection*

Below: Some roadside stations only had platforms serving the passenger or, as they were sometimes called, fast lines (on the GWR they were known as main lines). This example shows a station with two platform faces on the fast lines with the goods lines passing behind it. I have assumed that passenger trains do not run over the goods lines, but there it is a crossover where Up goods trains could be 'turned out' to run on the main line and Down goods trains be 'turned inside' off the fast line. The two trailing crossovers and connections on the goods lines would apply only if there were a goods yard.

Bottom: This is Berkhamsted on the London to Birmingham line of the LNWR, now commonly described as the West Coast Main Line. It represents an important main-line roadside station where there is a considerable amount of traffic. There are four running lines: the pairs of Up and Down fast and slow lines are separated by an island platform, with outer platforms providing four faces in all. Access to the station is on the Down side, with a subway to enable passengers to reach the other three platform faces.

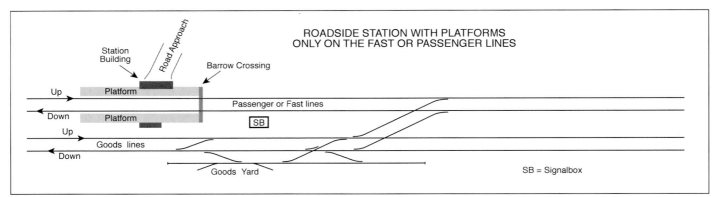

ROADSIDE STATION WITH PLATFORMS
ONLY ON THE FAST OR PASSENGER LINES

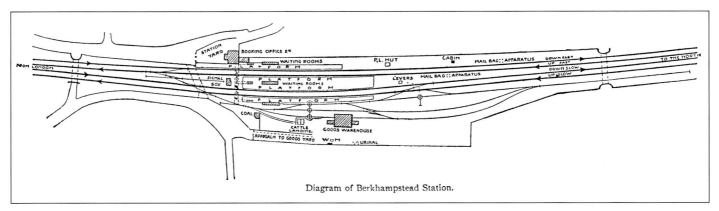

Diagram of Berkhampstead Station.

Large Suburban Stations

Many stations in this category had no goods facilities. Because the station was in a large town or city, the railway company found it more convenient to separate passenger and goods facilities and build two separate stations. Indeed, the goods station might serve an area that included a number of passenger stations. They could have two conventional line-side platforms or a single 'island' platform between the tracks, or a combination of both, providing four platform faces. Illustrations of a number of variations of this type of station have been included.

Top: There were two stations at Maryhill in Glasgow, and this late-1950s view shows the old Caledonian Railway station. Overlooked by three-storey dwellings and built in a cutting, this station is representative of large non-terminal stations in major cities and towns. To the right, in the bay platform, 2-6-4T No 42203 stands at the head of an 'Ordinary' passenger train. *R. S. Carpenter*

Above right: The ex-GNR/L&YR (Halifax & Ovenden Joint Line) station at North Bridge Halifax was overlooked by both industrial buildings and houses. The station was closed to passenger traffic on 23 May 1955, three days before this picture was taken, but I felt that it was worth including in order to illustrate a suburban station in an industrial area during the British Railways period. *H. B. Priestley*

Right: In addition to the main-line terminal station at King's Cross, there was also a Metropolitan Railway station that handled passenger trains. Opened in 1863 as King's Cross Met, it was renamed King's Cross & St Pancras in 1925, 11 years before this picture of No 22 was taken. *H. F. Wheeller*

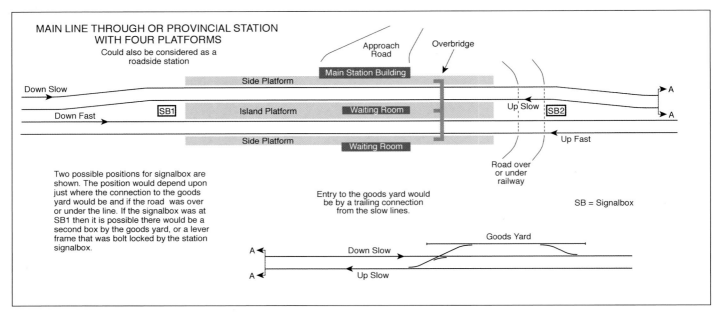

MAIN LINE THROUGH OR PROVINCIAL STATION
WITH FOUR PLATFORMS
Could also be considered as a
roadside station

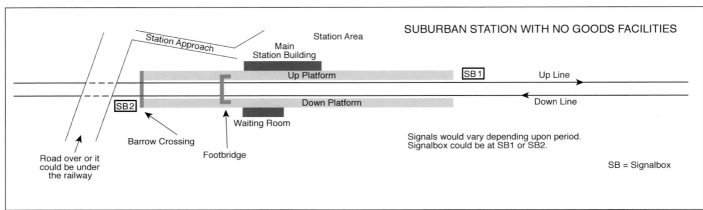

SUBURBAN STATION WITH NO GOODS FACILITIES

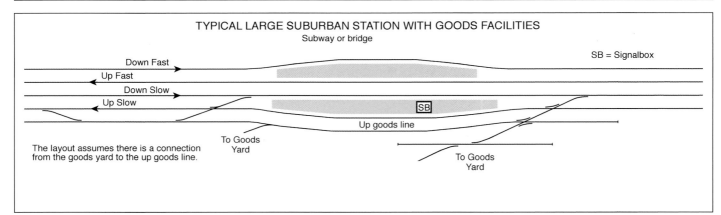

TYPICAL LARGE SUBURBAN STATION WITH GOODS FACILITIES
Subway or bridge

Top: This plan shows a station with four platform faces; facing connections could be added between the Up or Down Fast to Slow or Slow to Fast lines. Two possible positions are shown for the signalbox, which would depend upon access to any goods facilities that might be provided, while the sighting under the road bridge would be a factor in position 2, but not if the road was below the railway. In the section beyond 'AA' I have suggested one way of incorporating a goods yard, but it could equally well be at the other end of the station.

Centre: I consider this to be a very typical suburban station without goods facilities, again with two alternative positions for the signalbox. The road approach to stations of this type might be from a bridge as shown, with the road entrance below road level, or on the same level.

Above: This example shows a four-track double-island station with four platform faces and an outside Up goods line that connects to the goods yard. The road entrance might be on the far side opposite the goods yard, which would have a separate entrance, with passengers gaining access to the platforms by either a subway or overbridge.

Through Provincial Stations

This class of station could be a through station, but it was usual also to find bay platforms as well as the through platforms. They were often built as large island platforms or as two islands, one to serve Up and the other Down trains. Many could also be classified as junction stations, and this perhaps helps to explain why the LMS manual did not have a separate category for the latter. A track plan of a large station, which is also a junction, has been included, together with a number of illustrations to show the variety that existed.

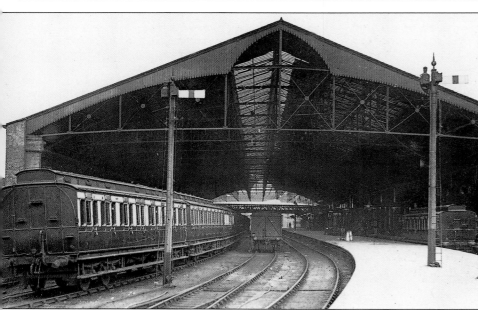

Above: This picture of the old Midland Railway Derby station was probably taken about 1938, but it could be post-World War 2. No 1327 and the three carriages may be a train that has been shunted 'out of the way' rather than being left standing on a through platform line, or more likely some 'strengthening' vehicles that will be attached to another train; some labels can be seen on the windows of the ex-Midland Railway Brake Third coupled to the locomotive, and on the first compartment of the centre coach. Whatever the case, the picture provides a pleasant view of Derby station during the steam era. *T. G. Hepburn/Rail Archive Stephenson*

Left: There were two major stations in Wolverhampton: the LNWR's high-level station and the GWR's low-level facility, featured in this undated picture. Although I think clerestory carriages are rather distinctive, this does not appear to be a view shared by many GWR modellers, as they are not very common on models of GWR lines. Note the safety or trap points at the end of the through road to protect the platform line from any vehicle that might 'run away'. *HMRS M13852*

Left: Shrewsbury General station had been jointly owned by the GWR and LMS, and this BR-period view from early 1960s provides a reminder of the period when steam power and diesels could be seen together. To the left, ex-GWR 4-6-0 'Manor' class No 7801 heads the 'Cambrian Coast Express', in the centre ex-LMS 2-6-2T No 40205 is making a lot of steam, while to the right we can see a DMU. *Mile Post 92½/A. W. V. Mace*

Right: The Highland and Great North of Scotland railway companies owned separate stations in Elgin, and this picture, taken on 21 July 1954, illustrates the old GNoSR station, on the line between Lossiemouth and Craigellachie. The longevity of carriages built before 1923 can also be seen in this picture: at least one of the vehicles seen on the right is pre-Grouping. *Author's collection*

Above: When this picture was taken on 15 April 1949 the station at Aberdeen was still known as Aberdeen Joint, but in 1952 'Joint' was removed from the name. Originally owned by the Caledonian and Great North of Scotland companies (later LMS and LNER), it provides further proof that modellers of the pre-1948 period do not have to be confined to a single company. Ex-LNER Class B12 4-6-0 No 61505 is on what appears to be a passenger train, even though the locomotive is not carrying the correct headlamp code. *J. F. Henton*

Centre right: Although it is probably unlikely that anyone would build a model of Rugby, I have included this track plan because it includes elements that could be incorporated into other station layouts. Rugby is a large island station, and this layout offers many advantages. Its one big platform area provides economies of staff, who can move quickly to where they are required. There is one booking office and one refreshment room, with entrance doors on both sides of the building — in effect two separate rooms divided by a full-length counter. When a station of this type is also a junction, and many were, the island layout is of immense help to passengers changing trains, to say nothing of the staff who might be transferring parcel traffic from one train to another. One disadvantage might be possible speed restrictions for any fast through trains if the curves are sharp.

The bay platforms at the north and south end enable passenger train services to be worked to a variety of destinations. At Rugby, trains arrived at the south end from London, Northampton, Stamford, Peterborough and beyond, while at the north end the arrivals came from Leamington, Birmingham, Stafford and Leicester, with corresponding departures. The arrangement of 'scissors' crossovers on both the Up and Down platforms allowed two trains to stand one behind the other and the rear train to start first. Note that the Stamford, Peterborough and Leicester trains arrived at and departed from the bay platforms. Finally, crossovers in the bay platforms allowed an incoming engine to run round its stock. In my view anyone seeking to build a model of this type of station should study the arrangements at Rugby in order to see what features they could incorporate into their model.

Below: A view of Marthwaite taken from the Down platform looking towards the signalbox and beyond to the tunnel. The signal arm on the right of the bracket controlled the exit from the bay and the other was for 'turnback' trains that arrived on the Up line and returned in the Down direction, crossing from Up to Down lines by using the crossover. The Ordinary passenger train is headed by 4-4-0 No 773. *Tony Wright*

Right: This through provincial station has two bay platforms, each with a platform road and outside siding. Passenger trains terminating in the Down platform could be set back into the Up sidings, the engine released and the carriages gravity shunted into the Up bay platform as described in *Railway Operation for the Modeller*, or the stock could be run round and propelled back into the bay, allowing the engine to work it away on a return journey. The Down bay could also be used for originating/terminating trains, but most of the passenger traffic would be through trains that stopped at the station. The goods lines are away from the station area and the goods station is connected to them. Finally, note that there would probably be two signalboxes.

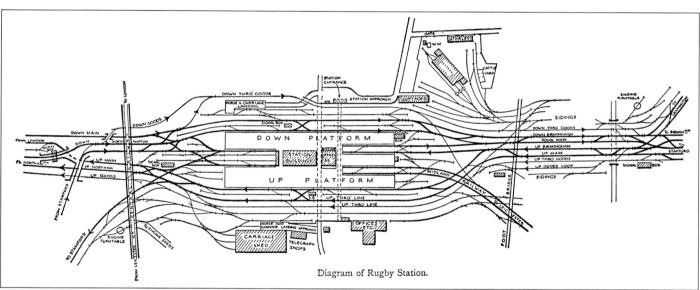

Diagram of Rugby Station.

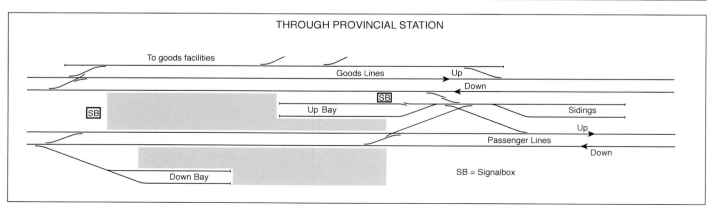

THROUGH PROVINCIAL STATION

SB = Signalbox

Terminal Stations

This class of station varied from the very large to the very small, but they shared a common feature: they were all at the end of the line (or almost at the end, as in some cases the line beyond the end of the platform became a siding). In its simplest form, the terminal station was no more than a single platform face with a run-round, or there could be one or two goods sidings. Modellers often place the engine shed for the branch engine at a small terminal station, and while this was not uncommon, where space is at a premium it is worth remembering that many branch engines worked from sheds at the junction.

At the other extreme, terminal stations could be very large, and a track plan of one of the larger city terminals has been included.

Some terminal stations were rather unusual in that trains ran in, then reversed out to take a different route. Examples include Lydham Heath (Bishop's Castle Railway); Lanark (CR); Colchester (GER); Barnstaple Victoria Road, Bodmin General, Coombe Junction and Swansea High Street, where probably a fresh engine was provided (all GWR); Brighton and Eastbourne (LB&SCR), where also a fresh engine was probably provided; Morecambe Promenade, for Heysham trains (MR); Fort William (NBR), where again a fresh engine was probably provided; and Cannon Street (SE&CR), also probably using a fresh engine. Where no fresh engine was provided, all run-round movements were controlled by signals (usually ground or disc signals), with in some cases a separate ground frame bolt-locked and released from the signalbox. At Lydham Heath there was a lever stand or ground frame to unlock the points, but no signals.

While dealing with unusual train movements, there were at least four non-terminal stations where trains ran round under the control of signals before departing on different routes; these were Connel Ferry (CR), and Battersby Junction, Tweedmouth and Whitby West Cliff (all NER).

Below: Because terminal stations are rather popular with modellers I have used pictures of more modest-sized stations in this section, but I could not resist including one city terminus. This undated but pre-1912 view of the Great Eastern station at Fenchurch Street illustrates a station that was owned by the GER but was also the London terminus of the London, Tilbury & Southend Railway. Note the Great Eastern engine on the short engine siding between the two platform lines, a common arrangement at terminal stations. I presume that LT&SR 4-4-2T No 57 on the right has arrived with a passenger train, which has been drawn clear to allow the locomotive to take up its next working, which, judging by the headboard, will be to Southend. Finally, it is worth noting the variety of poster advertising boards, very typical of this period. *Author's collection*

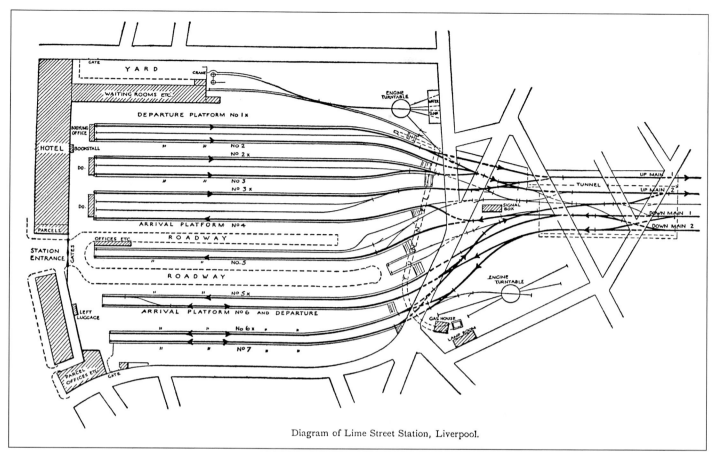

Diagram of Lime Street Station, Liverpool.

Above: This plan of Liverpool Lime Street station was included in the 1912 book *Modern Railway Working* (see the Bibliography) and I have adapted the description written more than 90 years ago, in which the platforms were described as 'semi island', seven in number parallel to each other and open at the ends. Three were allotted to departing trains, two to incoming trains, and two used for either.

Most of the trains arriving at the station, other than permanently coupled local ('residential') sets, were drawn out by a shunting engine (station pilot) and taken to Edge Hill, about a mile away, for re-marshalling if necessary and cleaning and examination before being brought back to the station to work the next service rostered for the set. Trains that did not require re-marshalling were run into one of the platforms that were used for both arrivals and departures, using the train engine that had worked the train to Lime Street. The sets did not remain at the platform too long and a fresh engine would be coupled to the departure end of the carriages. When the train departed, the engine that had been trapped at the end of the platform was able to follow the coaches and take up its next duty, be it to go to the engine shed or locomotive yard or to be coupled to another set of carriages.

The site of Lime Street is cramped but there are elements that modellers could incorporate into a model of a major city terminal, although two engine servicing points, each with a turntable, may be considered as being one too many!

Above: On a more modest scale, Caterham was the terminus of the South Eastern & Chatham Railway branch from Purley, and by the time this Southern Railway-period picture was taken the line had been electrified for passenger trains. *R. Cogger*

Top right: Newport Pagnell was the terminus of the LNWR branch line from Wolverton. This picture was taken on 3 September 1964, just before the station was closed to traffic, and shows a motor train worked by 2-6-2T No 41222. In the section about signalling in *Railway Operation for the Modeller* I drew attention to the fact that not every station had a signalbox and that at some stations the points and signals were worked from a stage or ground frame, which was on the station platform. An example of this practice can be seen here. *Millbrook House Ltd*

Above: A picture of Kendal Castle taken at eye level along the platform; the effect is most realistic. Ex-Midland Railway 'Belpaire' No 773 is at the head of an Ordinary passenger train with the model of the Midland Railway coaling stage to the right. Perhaps all that is missing is the driver leaning out of the cab waiting for the 'right away'. *Tony Wright*

Above left: An overall view of the station at Kendal Castle with No 13004 waiting to depart with the Up 'Dalesman Express'. The overall scene is one of activity: three engines on shed with another behind the signalbox, which appears to be setting back onto the carriages at the end of the platform. There is another engine in the side and end milk and parcels dock, which is placed between the station and the engine shed, and finally one at the head of the train on the platform on the right of the picture. *Tony Wright*

Left: Ongar was the terminus of the Great Eastern Railway's branch from Stratford, and this undated view shows the station area during the LNER period. A small passenger station with a goods yard and locomotive shed, it represents an ideal prototype for modellers interested in branch terminal stations. Passenger trains were largely worked by small Class F6 2-4-2T engines, and Nos 7069 and 7067 can be seen on the left. The carriages are standing by a side- and end-loading dock, which also dealt with cattle. I would expect the sidings between the loading dock and the goods shed to have been used to store coaches. *W. A. Camwell*

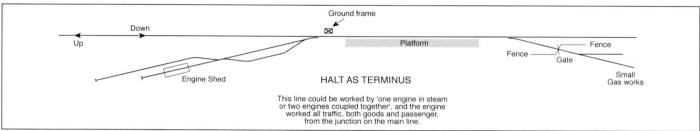

Down

Up

Ground frame

Platform

Fence

Fence — | — Gate

Small
Gas works

Engine Shed

HALT AS TERMINUS

This line could be worked by 'one engine in steam
or two engines coupled together', and the engine
worked all traffic, both goods and passenger,
from the junction on the main line.

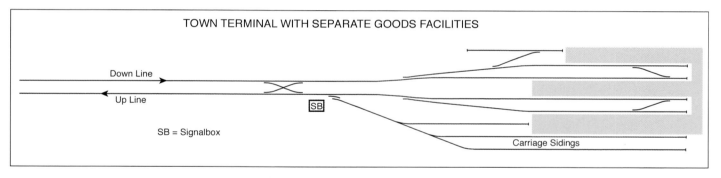

TOWN TERMINAL WITH SEPARATE GOODS FACILITIES

Down Line

Up Line

SB = Signalbox

Carriage Sidings

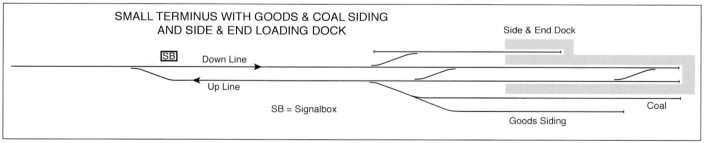

**SMALL TERMINUS WITH GOODS & COAL SIDING
AND SIDE & END LOADING DOCK**

Side & End Dock

Down Line

Up Line

SB = Signalbox

Coal

Goods Siding

Centre above: This is a halt that also serves as a terminus at the end of a branch worked by 'one engine in steam or two engines coupled together'. Therefore no signals are required, but there is a ground frame that is unlocked by the train staff. A tank engine kept at the terminus works this branch and the carriage stock is stabled on the loop by the engine shed. There is a run-round loop within the gasworks sidings, and all traffic to and from the works is handled by the railway company engine.

Centre below: This town terminal passenger station is separate from the goods station, which is further along the line. There are three platform faces used by passenger trains, while the short platform is for parcels traffic, where there is also an end-loading dock. The short siding near the carriage sidings is used for locomotive purposes. The 'scissors' crossover by the signalbox enables incoming trains to run into any platform, and the same applies to departing trains. A small engine shed is assumed to be close to the goods station, which means that light engine movements will be necessary to enable tender locomotives to be turned before the return working.

Above: This is a simplified version of the previous plan, but with some limited goods facilities at the passenger terminus; depending upon space, these could be enlarged and further sidings added. Passenger trains will arrive at the Down platform and the carriages put into the Up platform, allowing another train to arrive while the carriages from the first are still in the station; alternatively, the engine could run round and depart from the Down platform. An engine turntable could be added if the line was not worked by tank engines.

Above: Cromer Beach was the M&GNJR station in Cromer — there was also a Great Eastern station — and by means of a triangle less than a mile from the station trains could run either west towards Sheringham and Melton Constable or east towards Mundesley. This picture, taken on 7 June 1952, shows ex-GER Class D16 No 62533 on an 'Ordinary' passenger train made up of three coaches and forming the 7.25pm Cromer Beach to Melton Constable service. *Author's collection*

Right: Bordon was the terminus of the London & South Western Railway's branch from Bentley in Hampshire. This picture was taken on 15 October 1947, just prior to Nationalisation, and shows the 5.10pm motor train to Bentley, hauled by ex-LSWR 0-4-4T No 108. *W. A. Camwell*

Centre right: The principal station at Romford was on the Great Eastern Railway line from London to Southend, but in 1893 the LT&SR built a branch from Upminster, terminating at the platform seen here. Originally there was a rail connection between the lines of the two companies, but this was removed in 1931 and restored in 1940. The Midland signalbox was closed in 1936 and a key on the single-line tablet released the single point hand lever that allowed the points for the crossover to be reversed. During the 1930s the entrance to the old LT&SR station, by now owned by the LMS, was closed and the station combined with the LNER station. I mention this to show that over the years changes took place and some could be incorporated into models. *Author's collection*

Below right: Banff was the terminus of the Great North of Scotland Railway branch from Tillynaught, and this 22 July 1954 picture shows ex-GNoSR 4-4-0 No 62262 about to work the 2.45pm Banff to Tillynaught 'Ordinary' passenger train. The locomotive is dual-fitted — both vacuum and Westinghouse brake hoses can be seen — but the lamp code has not been set, unless things were done differently in the far north of Scotland!
T. J. Edgington

Dock Stations

This class of station is usually associated with seaports where passengers were either embarking or disembarking from ocean liners or ferries, but there were also a few stations close to areas of inland water where passengers boarded lake steamers, generally for pleasure purposes. A good example is the Furness Railway station at Windermere Lakeside. For those modellers who may be attracted to this type of layout, it is worth pointing out that the railway companies also owned a number of ships and these could be an important feature of a model based upon this idea. Other examples of this type of station are Balloch Pier (Dumbarton & Balloch Joint [Caledonian & North British]), Loch Tay (CR) and Banavie Pier (NBR). Finally we should not forget the train ferry terminal at Dover Western Docks.

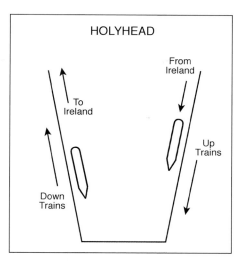

HOLYHEAD

To Ireland

From Ireland

Down Trains

Up Trains

Left: It proved very difficult to find a 'typical' dock station layout, so I have included a sketch to show the layout at Holyhead, where ships arrived on the east side and were moved to the west side for departure, leaving stern-first. Arrangements at some other docks were as follows: at Heysham Harbour, ships berthed at the south wall parallel to the trains; at Fishguard Harbour they berthed on the west wall parallel to the trains; at Fleetwood, Weymouth, Newhaven and Harwich, which were all on rivers, ships also berthed parallel to trains; at Dover and Folkestone the piers were on the outer walls of the harbour, and trains ran on to the piers parallel to the ships; at Portsmouth Harbour boats berthed across the end of the pier at right angles to the station; and at Ryde Pier Head there were berths on three sides of the pier head.

Below: Unlike the other classes of stations described in this chapter, I found that other than the fact that passengers transferred from water to rail or vice versa, there was little in common between the various types of dock station that would be helpful to modellers. This probably accounts for the fact that any form of dock passenger station is a rarity as the subject for a model railway. One of the major ports for Irish traffic is Holyhead, so I have included two pictures of this dock station. The first, undated, view shows the paddle steamer *Banshee* with the passenger station in the background. *Author's collection*

Right: This picture, believed to date from 1909, provides a view of the quayside and the station platform. A note on the rear of the print states 'Holyhead train quay and tender PS [paddle steamer] *Edith*'. *Author's collection*

Right: The station sign for the Mersey Docks & Harbour Board station at Liverpool Riverside is shown in this 1959 picture. *T. J. Edgington*

Below: Wemyss Bay was the terminus of the Caledonian Railway branch from Port Glasgow, and this 1968 picture provides a general view of the station in relation to the ships, although not much of the railway can be seen. *T. J. Edgington*

Left: Although junction stations were not shown as a separate category in the LMS's 1938 publication *Passenger Station Working*, I felt that I ought to illustrate some; although they could also be described as roadside stations, the LMS classification is not, in my view, very precise. Afon Wen was on the old Cambrian Railways line from Portmadoc to Pwllheli, and was also the junction for LNWR trains from Caernarvon. This undated British Railways-period picture shows an Ivatt Class 2MT with a reporting number on the smokebox and a 2-6-4T on an 'Ordinary' passenger train.
Author's collection

Below: This undated picture, looking east, shows the Great Eastern station at Stepney, with the line to Bow Junction on the left and the branch to Blackwall on the right.
Author's collection

Junction Stations

A junction is, of course, where two or more lines come together, and the size of junction stations varied immensely. At one extreme there was Crewe, probably the most famous of them all, and at the other stations like Broom in Warwickshire. The latter station was on a north-south single line with a passing loop, which was owned by the Midland Railway, but was junction for another single line from the east, the S&MJR, which joined the MR south of the station. In model terms it is more likely to be a 'Broom' than a 'Crewe', but notwithstanding their size junction stations shared common features: each was a place where some passengers would

change trains, where through coaches could be transferred from one train to another, and where engines might be changed. At some junctions all the lines belonged to the same company; at others more than one company was involved. When this happened the arrangement could vary from one company granting running powers to the other, to the area being jointly owned — Carlisle Citadel is probably the best example of the latter, being jointly owned by the Caledonian and LNWR, with the NER, GSWR, MR, M&CR and NBR as 'tenants in common', in other words they enjoyed running powers and worked their own trains. In my view all junction stations offer modellers scope for building distinctive models.

One delightful feature of some junction stations was the bay or side platform where a branch passenger train arrived to await the arrival of the main-line train. On the model the latter arrives, and in our imagination the passengers from stations served by the branch train board it, while passengers from the through train alight with their luggage and perhaps board the branch train. In due course the main-line train departs, to be followed by the branch train.

Junction stations often, but not always, had locomotive facilities. If we take our examples of 'Broom' and 'Crewe', we find that at Broom there was an engine turntable, but at Crewe there were two major locomotive depots.

Above: The former Highland Railway station at The Mound was the junction for the lines from Dornoch, Dingwall and Thurso. The station was built on a gradient and the line to Dornoch, on the right, has a platform at a lower level than the one that served Thurso line trains. *P. J. Garland*

Below: Junctions do not have to be on multi-track main lines, and this picture of Glastonbury station, taken on 17 August 1965, has been included to make this point. To the right of the picture can be seen part of the Wells branch, which closed in 1951, although the connection between the branch and main line remained. Although on a single line with a passing loop, there were considerable goods facilities at Glastonbury, and readers interested in S&DJR stations are strongly recommended to read *An Historical Survey of the Somerset & Dorset Railway* by Judge and Potts (see the Bibliography), which includes detailed track plans for all stations. The train is the 9.45am Highbridge to Templecombe service, behind 2-6-2T No 41291. *Paul Cotterell*

Right top to bottom:
This plan shows a main-line station that is also the junction for a short branch line. The engine shed is at the branch terminal and the branch is worked under 'one engine in steam' regulations, with one locomotive handling all traffic, both passenger and freight. On the main line express trains do not stop, but there is a service of 'Ordinary' passenger trains that call, and most connect with the branch passenger service. Goods traffic is detached from trains on the main line and left on the lay-by or Up siding, being picked up by the branch engine, which also leaves traffic that has originated on the branch to be collected by through freight trains.

This double-line junction station has a level crossing and two sidings that could be refuge sidings or used for detaching or attaching traffic to or from the branch. The goods facilities could be extended and additional sidings added on either or both sides of the line.

This is a typical track layout for a junction between two single lines, with a passing loop and some goods facilities; it could be used by two different companies or just one. It would be possible for a passenger train to arrive from line B and to stand in the loop-line platform while a passenger train ran through on line A. If the train from line B arrived first, passengers who wished to join the train on line A would cross over to the platform before it arrived, while passengers from the train on line A would wait until their train had departed before crossing the line to join the other train, which would return on line B.

Some junction stations had turntables to enable engines to be turned. Here is an example of a junction where two double lines meet and where there is an engine turntable. In addition there is a Down goods loop and siding, and a bay platform where a branch passenger train could stand between trips. If it was a motor train there would be no need to run round, but facilities exist if required. If a tender engine was used for passenger traffic, the turntable would be used, but it would probably be quite small and a relic from the period before motor trains were introduced.

Within this category could be included those stations where trains ran past and reversed in, then departed to continue their journeys. Some recorded by me are: Dudley (GWR), involving diesel railcars and steam auto-trains from Birmingham Snow Hill; Inverness (HR), where trains from the south backed in to connect with Wick or Kyle trains;. Newport (Isle of Wight Central Railway/SR/BR), for Freshwater trains (SR and BR); Guisborough and Saltburn (NER), for trains on the two respective lines between Whitby and Middlesbrough; and Dorchester (LSWR), for Up trains only.

A variation of this was to be found at Malton (NER) between the station and Scarborough

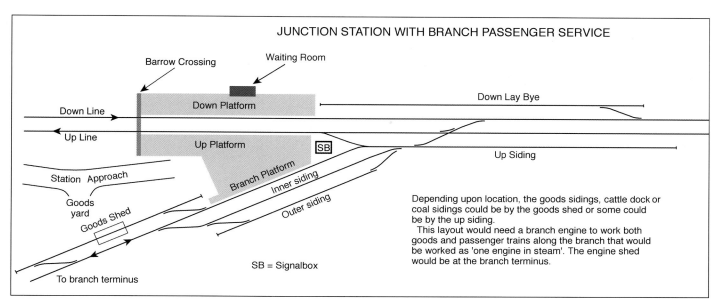

JUNCTION STATION WITH BRANCH PASSENGER SERVICE

Barrow Crossing

Waiting Room

Down Platform

Down Lay Bye

Down Line

Up Line

Up Platform

SB

Up Siding

Station Approach

Branch Platform

Inner siding

Outer siding

Goods yard

Goods Shed

To branch terminus

SB = Signalbox

Depending upon location, the goods sidings, cattle dock or coal sidings could be by the goods shed or some could be by the up siding.
  This layout would need a branch engine to work both goods and passenger trains along the branch that would be worked as 'one engine in steam'. The engine shed would be at the branch terminus.

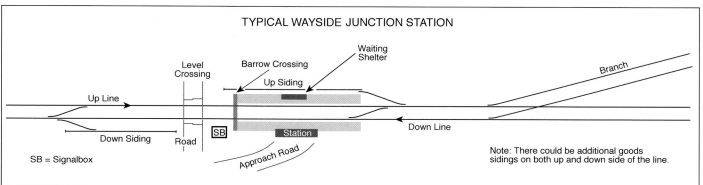

TYPICAL WAYSIDE JUNCTION STATION

Waiting Shelter

Level Crossing

Barrow Crossing

Up Siding

Branch

Up Line

Down Siding

Road

SB

Station

Down Line

SB = Signalbox

Approach Road

Note: There could be additional goods sidings on both up and down side of the line.

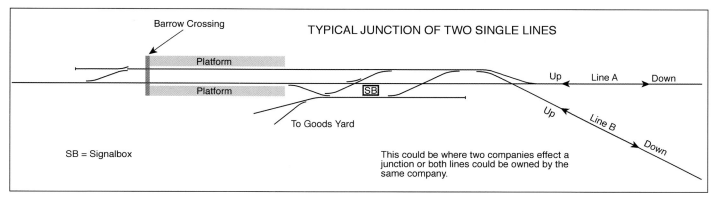

Barrow Crossing

TYPICAL JUNCTION OF TWO SINGLE LINES

Platform

Platform

Up   Line A   Down

SB

To Goods Yard

Up   Line B

Down

SB = Signalbox

This could be where two companies effect a junction or both lines could be owned by the same company.

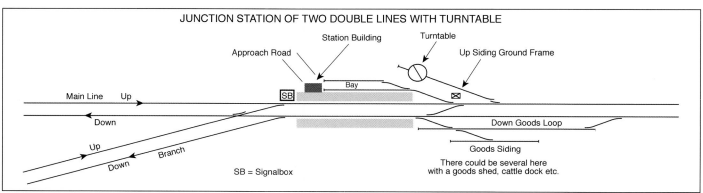

JUNCTION STATION OF TWO DOUBLE LINES WITH TURNTABLE

Station Building

Turntable

Approach Road

Up Siding Ground Frame

Main Line   Up

SB

Bay

Down

Down Goods Loop

Up

Down   Branch

Goods Siding

There could be several here with a goods shed, cattle dock etc.

SB = Signalbox

Road Junction; trains to and from the station had a pilot engine at one end. The same system was used between Templecombe's S&DJR and LSWR stations.

Other types of station need to be mentioned, and they generally came within the 'roadside' category. These were 'high-level' and 'low-level' stations, as at Tamworth, a plan of which is included. There were also high-level and low-level stations at Dudley Port and Wolverhampton. Some stations existed only for racecourse traffic, as at Cheltenham and Newbury on the GWR and Bromford Bridge on the Midland. Finally, we should not forget triangular stations, some of which are still open. Examples include Ambergate (MR), Rutherglen (CR), Forres (HR), Queensbury (GNR), Earlestown (LNWR), Bishop Auckland (NER) and Shipley (MR); the latter became a triangular station under British Railways ownership.

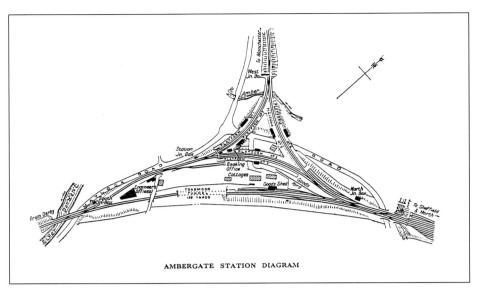

AMBERGATE STATION DIAGRAM

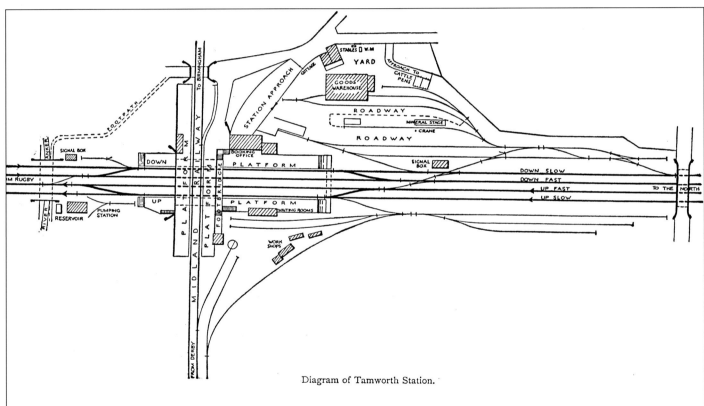

Diagram of Tamworth Station.

Top right: Although triangular stations were rather rare, they did exist and at least one model of such a station has been built. I have therefore included this track plan of Ambergate in the hope that it will inspire others to build models of this form of station. Note that through trains running between Derby and Sheffield, which were not scheduled to stop at the station, ran via Toadmoor Tunnel and avoided the station entirely. The 4mm-scale model of Ambergate captures the atmosphere of the prototype, although the space required is beyond the reach of many modellers.

Above: Tamworth was rather unusual. Before the 1923 Grouping the high-level station was owned by the Midland Railway and the larger low-level station by the LNWR, but from 1923 the entire station belonged to the LMS. In *Modern Railway Working* of 1912 the low-level station was described as 'a modern roadside station on a main line which consists of four lines of rails, two of which are "fast lines" and two "slow lines"'. The plan shows the station layout prior to the Great War and, although not

shown, north of the station the lines were reduced from four to two; also, during the Grouping period the arrangement of the low-level station signalboxes was altered. The high-level station signalbox was at the end of the footbridge, close to the turntable.

Note that there are only two low-level platform faces, both on the slow lines, which meant that stopping trains ran on the slow lines and express trains on the fast lines. However, the arrangement of the crossovers meant that trains on the fast lines could gain the slow lines and stop at the platforms before regaining the fast lines if required. The arrangement of the station approach and the LNWR goods yard provides readers with a very good example of how this might be done. What makes this station rather unusual is the connection with the high-level Midland Railway station; however, because it did not involve passenger traffic, it is not within the terms of reference for this book. Of course, either station could be used in isolation as an example of a main-line roadside station.

Postscript

During the short period of time between completing this work and delivering it to the publisher I found myself reflecting upon what I had sought to achieve and wondering if it had been realised. You the reader will make the final judgement, and if some of the ideas and suggestions set out in this work begin to appear on model railways, then I will be able to say that it was worth while.

Over the years my ideas have changed; at first my models of stations had no basis in reality but were based on the concept 'it might have been but never was'. There are two problems with this approach: one is the 'no one knows whether it's correct or not' or 'modellers' licence' claim, which could also be described as being slapdash, and the second is that it takes much longer to work out what might have happened if the line had been built. However, one advantage of building an imaginary layout is that you learn a lot about the subject you are modelling, proving that research in its own right is very rewarding indeed.

My approach today is to model an actual location or, if that is not possible, to try to find one that reflects what I want, but may not have belonged to the same company as on the model. The entire thrust of this book has been to try to show that the principles described applied to all British railways — it was only the detail that varied. The main thing is to attempt to reproduce the essential features in order to capture the flavour of the full-size railway, rather than try to squeeze in something that will not fit the space you have available, and in so doing be forced to omit some essential features to be found on the prototype.

Above: A rather splendid picture of No 5902, also shown on page 19, shows it carrying express passenger train headlamps while entering Marthwaite station with an Up train. Note the ground signal for setting back shunting moves that were a feature of this station's operating procedure (see page 33 where a shunting move is taking place). *Tony Wright*

Left: It seems only right to conclude with this picture of Midland 4-4-0 No 2184 at the head of one of David's Midland trains, which, because they were out of period with his layout were known as the 'Funny Trains'. When I used to visit him I was quite happy to see this train run round and round while enjoying the spectacle. At the risk of repeating what I have said before, only well-made and -operated models can recreate the image of the steam railway of yesteryear and on this layout you could capture the flavour of the age of the steam railway, in particular the passenger trains. *Tony Wright*

Bibliography, References and Sources

Works referred to in the text

Ahrons, E. L., *The British Railway Steam Locomotive 1825-1925* (Locomotive Publishing Company, 1927; Bracken Books, 1987)

Braithwaite, Jack, *Midland Record 15: The Johnson Bogie Singles* (Wild Swan Publications, 2000)

Cameron, T. F., *An Outline of Railway Traffic Operation* (Railway Publishing Company, 1946)

Essery, Bob, *Ashchurch to Barnt Green Line: The Evesham Route* (OPC, 2002)

Essery, Bob, *British Railway Modelling Special: Classic Layouts* (Warners Group, 2001)

Essery, Bob, *Railway Operation for the Modeller* (Midland Publishing, 2003)

Essery, Bob and Lane, Barry, *Midland Record 18: Carriage Cleaning* (Wild Swan Publications, 2003)

Essery, R. J., *An Illustrated History of Midland Wagons* Volumes 1 & 2 (OPC, 1980)

Essery, Bob, *Railway Archive No 4: The Civil Engineering of the Chapeltown Branch* (2003)

Essery, Bob, *Railway Archive No 4: The Civil Engineering of the Chapeltown Branch* (2003)

London, Tilbury & Southend Railway and its Locomotives (OPC, 2001)

Fryer, C. E. J., *A History of Slipping and Slip Carriages* (The Oakwood Press, 1997)

Hare, T. Bernard, *British Railway Operation* (Modern Transport Publishing Co Ltd, 1930)

Harris, Michael, *Great Western Coaches from 1890* (David & Charles, 1966; David St John Thomas, 1993)

Jackson, Jim, *Southwell Engineman* (LMS Journal Preview, Wild Swan Publications, 2001)

Jenkinson, David, *British Railway Carriages of the 20th Century* (Patrick Stephens Ltd, Volume 1 1988, Volume 2 1990)

LMS School of Transport *Passenger Station Working* (1938)

Macaulay, John (ed), *Modern Railway Working* Volume 1 (The Gresham Publishing Company, 1912)

Mullay, A. J., *Streamlined Steam* (David & Charles, 1994)

Nock, O. S., *British Locomotives of the 20th Century* Volume 1 (Patrick Stephens Ltd, 1983)

Pearson, Rod, *The Bass Railway Trips* (Breedon Books Publishing Company Ltd, 1993)

Wood, L. V., *Bridges for Modellers* (OPC, 1985)

Other references used

General Appendix to the Working Time Table, various editions

Carriage Marshalling Books, various editions

Readers are recommended to refer to the following carriage books for details of the stock of specific companies:

LMS Group

Essery, R. J. and Jenkinson, D., *The LMS Coach* (Ian Allan, 1969)

Jenkinson, David, *Historic Carriage Drawings* Volume 2 (The Pendragon Partnership, 1998)

Jenkinson, D. and Essery, R. J., *LMS Coaches: An Illustrated History* (OPC, 1977)

Midland Carriages: An Illustrated Review (OPC, 1984)

The Illustrated History of LMS Standard Coaching Stock (OPC, Volume 1 1991, Volume 2 1994, Volume 3 2000)

Lacy, R. E. and Dow, George, *Midland Railway Carriages* (Wild Swan Publications, Volume 1 1984, Volume 2 1986)

Radford, J. B., *The American Pullman Cars of the Midland Railway* (Ian Allan, 1984)

Rush, R. W., *Furness Railway Locomotives and Rolling Stock* (The Oakwood Press, nd)

LNER Group

Harris, Michael, *LNER Carriages* (Atlantic Transport Publishers, 1994, 1995)

Great Northern Railway and East Coast Joint Stock Carriages from 1905 (The Oakwood Press)

GWR Group

Harris, Michael, *Great Western Coaches from 1890* (David & Charles, 1966; David St John Thomas, 1993)

Lewis, John, *Official Drawings No 3: Great Western Coaches* (Wild Swan Publications, 1998)

Russell, J. H., *Great Western Coaches 1903-48, Appendix: Vol 1 Standard Passenger Stock* and *Vol 2: Specific Duty Coaches and the Brown Vehicles*, (OPC, 1973, 1981 and 1984)

Southern Group

King, Mike, *An Illustrated History of Southern Coaches* (OPC, 2003)

Weddell, G. R., *LSWR Carriages in the 20th Century* (OPC, 2001)

Independent

Cull, J. E. and Prigmore, B. J., *Mersey Railway Electric Stock* (Peter R. Davis, London, 1968)

British Railways

Parkin, Keith, *British Railways Mark 1 Coaches* (Pendragon/HMRS, 1991)

All companies

Behrend, George, *Pullman in Europe* (Ian Allan, 1962)

Jenkinson, David, *British Railway Carriages in the 20th Century* (Patrick Stephens Ltd, Volume 1 (1901-1922) 1988, Volume 2 (1923-1953) 1990)

Mullay, A. J., *Streamlined Steam* (David & Charles, 1994)

Tatlow, Peter, compiled by, *Historic Carriage Drawings* Volume 3 (The Pendragon Partnership, 2000)

Station layout plans

A number of books have been published over the years that provide details of signal and track plans that may be helpful to modellers who are planning station layouts. The selection given here is not complete, but will provide readers with an idea of what is available.

British Railways Layout Plans of the 1950s from the John Swift Collection, Volumes 1-18 (Signalling Record Society)

Hendry, Dr R. Preston and Powell, R., *An Historical Survey of Selected LMS Stations* (OPC, Volume 1 1982, Volume 2 1986)

Judge, C. W. and Potts, C. R., *An Historical Survey of the Somerset & Dorset Railway* (OPC, 1979)

Smith, Peter, *An Historical Survey of the Midland in Gloucestershire* (OPC, 1985)